MW00805033

First Print Edition [1.0] -1438 h. (2017 c.e.)

Copyright © 1438 H./2017 C.E.
Taalib al-Ilm Educational Resources

http://taalib.com
Learn Islaam, Live Islaam.^{SM}

Taalib al-Ilm Education Resources products are made available through distributors worldwide. To view a list of current distributors in your region, or information about our distributor/referral program please visit our website. Discounts on bulk quantities of our products are available to community groups, religious institutions, and other not-for-profit entities, inshAllaah. For details and discount information, contact the special sales department by e-mail: **service@taalib.com**.

The publisher requests that any corrections regarding translations or knowledge based issues, be sent to us at: **service@taalib.com.** Readers should note that internet web sites offered as citations and/or sources for further information may have changed or no longer be available between the time this was written and when it is read.

We publish a variety of full text and free preview edition electronic ebook formats. Some content that appears in print may not be available in electronic book versions.

ISBN EAN-13:   978-1-938117-32-9   [Soft cover Print Edition]

Golden Words Upon Golden Words…For Every Muslim.

"Imaam al-Barbahaaree, may Allaah have mercy upon him said:

May Allaah have mercy upon you! Examine carefully the speech of everyone you hear from in your time particularly. So do not act in haste and do not enter into anything from it until you ask and see: Did any of the Companions of the Prophet, may Allaah's praise and salutations be upon him, speak about it, or did any of the scholars? So if you find a narration from them about it, cling to it, do not go beyond it for anything and do not give precedence to anything over it and thus fall into the Fire.

Explanation by Sheikh Saaleh al-Fauzaan, may Allaah preserve him:

'Do not be hasty in accepting as correct what you may hear from the people, especially in these later times. As now there are many who speak about so many various matters, issuing rulings and ascribing to themselves both knowledge and the right to speak. This is especially the case after the emergence and spread of new modern day media technologies. Such that everyone now can speak and bring forth that which is, in truth, worthless; by this, meaning words of no true value - speaking about whatever they wish in the name of knowledge and in the name of the religion of Islaam. It has even reached the point that you find the people of misguidance and the members of the various groups of misguidance and deviance from the religion speaking as well. Such individuals have now become those who speak in the name of the religion of Islaam through means such as the various satellite television channels. Therefore be very cautious!

It is upon you, oh Muslim, and upon you, oh student of knowledge, individually, to verify matters and not rush to embrace everything and anything you may hear. It is upon you to verify the truth of what you hear, asking, 'Who else also makes this same statement or claim?', 'Where did this thought or concept originate or come from?', 'Who is its reference or source authority?' Asking what are the evidences which support it from within the Book and the Sunnah? And inquiring where has the individual who is putting this forth studied and taken his knowledge from? From who has he studied the knowledge of Islaam?

Each of these matters requires verification through inquiry and investigation, especially in the present age and time. It is not every speaker who should rightly be considered a source of knowledge, even if he is well spoken and eloquent and can manipulate words captivating his listeners. Do not be taken in and accept him until you are aware of the degree and scope of what he possesses of knowledge and understanding. Perhaps someone's words may be few, but possess true understanding, and perhaps another will have a great deal of speech yet he is actually ignorant to such a degree that he doesn't actually possess anything of true understanding. Rather he only has the ability to enchant with his speech so that the people are deceived. Yet he puts forth the perception that he is a scholar, that he is someone of true understanding and comprehension, that he is a capable thinker, and so forth. Through such means and ways he is able to deceive and beguile the people, taking them away from the way of truth.

Therefore, what is to be given true consideration is not the amount of the speech put forth or that one can extensively discuss a subject. Rather, the criterion that is to be given consideration is what that speech contains within it of sound authentic knowledge, what it contains of the established and transmitted principles of Islaam. Perhaps a short or brief statement which is connected to or has a foundation in the established principles can be of greater benefit than a great deal of speech which simply rambles on, and through hearing you don't actually receive very much benefit from.

This is the reality which is present in our time; one sees a tremendous amount of speech which only possesses within it a small amount of actual knowledge. We see the presence of many speakers, yet few people of true understanding and comprehension.' "

[The eminent major scholar Sheikh Saaleh al-Fauzaan, may Allaah preserve him- 'A Valued Gift for the Reader Of Comments Upon the Book Sharh as-Sunnah', page 102-103]

❧ *Is not He better than your so-called gods, He Who originates creation and shall then repeat it, and Who provides for you from heaven and earth? Is there any god with Allaah? Say: 'Bring forth your proofs, if you are truthful.'* ❧-(Surah an-Naml: 64)

Explanation: ❧ *Say: "Bring forth your proofs.."* ❧ This is a command for the Prophet, may Allaah's praise and salutation be upon him, to rebuke them immediately after they had put forward their own rebuke. Meaning: '*Say to them: bring your proof, whether it is an intellectual proof or a proof from transmitted knowledge, that would stand as evidence that there is another with Allaah, the Most Glorified and the Most Exalted*'. Additionally, it has been said that it means: '*Bring your proof that there is anyone other than Allaah, the Most High, who is capable of doing that which has been mentioned from His actions, the Most Glorified and the Most Exalted.*' ❧*...if you are truthful.*❧ meaning, in this claim. From this it is derived that a claim is not accepted unless clearly indicated by evidences."
   [Tafseer al-'Aloosee: vol. 15, page 14]

Sheikh Rabee'a Ibn Hadee Umair al-Madkhalee, may Allaah preserve him said,

'It is possible for someone to simply say, "*So and so said such and such.*" However we should say, "*Produce your proof.*" So why did you not ask them for their proof by saying to them: "*Where was this said?*" Ask them questions such as this, as from your weapons are such questions as: "*Where is this from? From which book? From which cassette?...*" '
   [The Overwhelming Falsehoods of 'Abdul-Lateef Bashmeel' page 14]

The guiding scholar Imaam Sheikh 'Abdul-'Azeez Ibn Abdullah Ibn Baaz, may Allaah have mercy upon him, said,

'It is not proper that any intelligent individual be misled or deceived by the great numbers from among people from the various countries who engage in such a practice. As the truth is not determined by the numerous people who engage in a matter, rather the truth is known by the Sharee'ah evidences. Just as Allaah the Most High says in Surah al-Baqarah, ❧ *And they say, "None shall enter Paradise unless he be a Jew or a Christian." These are only their own desires. Say "Produce your proof if you are truthful."* ❧-(Surah al-Baqarah: 111) And Allaah the Most High says ❧ *And if you obey most of those on the earth, they will mislead you far away from Allaah's path. They follow nothing but conjectures, and they do nothing but lie.* ❧-(Surah al-'Ana'an: 116)'
   [Collection of Rulings and Various Statements of Sheikh Ibn Baaz -Vol. 1 page 85]

Sheikh Muhammad Ibn 'Abdul-Wahaab, may Allaah have mercy upon him, said,

'Additionally, verify that knowledge held regarding your beliefs, distinguishing between what is correct and false within it, coming to understand the various areas of knowledge of faith in Allaah alone and the required disbelief in all other objects of worship. You will certainly see various different matters which are called towards and enjoined; so if you see that a matter is in fact one coming from Allaah and His Messenger, then this is what is intended and is desired that you possess. Otherwise, Allaah has certainly given you that which enables you to distinguish between truth and falsehood, if Allaah so wills.

Moreover, this writing of mine- do not conceal it from the author of that work; rather present it to him. He may repent and affirm its truthfulness and then return to the guidance of Allaah, or perhaps if he says that he has a proof for his claims, even if that is only a single statement, or if he claims that within my statements there is something unsupported, then request his evidence for that assertion. After this if there is something which continues to cause uncertainty or is a problem for you, then refer it back to me, so that then you are aware of both his statement and mine in that issue. We ask Allaah to guide us, you, and all the Muslims to that which He loves and is pleased with.'

[Personal Letters of Sheikh Muhammad Ibn 'Abdul-Wahaab- Conclusion to Letter 20]

Sheikh 'Abdullah Ibn 'Abdur-Rahman Abu Bateen, may Allaah have mercy upon him, said,

'And for an individual, if it becomes clear to him that something is the truth, he should not turn away from it and or be discouraged simply due to the few people who agree with him and the many who oppose him in that, especially in these latter days of this present age.

If the ignorant one says: "*If this was the truth so and so and so and so would have been aware of it!*" However this is the very claim of the disbelievers, in their statement found in the Qur'aan ❴ **If it had truly been good, they would not have preceded us to it!** ❵-(Surah al-Ahqaaf: 11) and in their statement ❴ **Is it these whom Allaah has favored from amongst us?** ❵-(Surah al-Ana'am: 53). Yet certainly, as Alee Ibn Abee Taalib, may Allaah be pleased with him, stated "*Know the truth and then you will know it' people.*" But for the one who generally stands upon confusion and uncertainty, then every doubt swirls around him. And if the majority of the people were in fact upon the truth today, then Islaam would not be considered strange, yet, by Allaah, it is today seen as the most strange of affairs!"

[Durar As-Sanneeyyah -vol. 10, page 400]

THE "30 DAYS OF GUIDANCE" SERIES

The goal of the "*30 Days of Guidance*" book series is to better enable us, as worshipers of Allaah, to embody and reflect in the various different areas of life for a Muslim, our connection and adherence to the believer's path of the first three believing generations. Many Muslims, due to lacking opportunities to study consistently and be cultivated at the feet of noble steadfast scholars, have an inconsistency they themselves recognize an inconsistency between the clear path of Islaam of the first Muslims, which they have connected themselves to, and what they have actually been successful in making a daily reality in their practice of Islaam. Sheikh Saaleh Ibn al-Fauzaan, may Allaah preserve him, explained the importance of striving to rectify this,

"... *For the one who proceeds upon the methodology of the best generations even if that is during the very last days of the existence of earth, then he is safe, saved, and protected from entering the Hellfire. As Allaah, the Most Glorified and the Most Exalted, said,* ⟨**And the first to embrace Islaam of the Muhaajiroon (those who migrated from Makkah to Al-Madinah) and the Ansaar (the citizens of Al-Madinah who helped and gave aid to the Muhaajiroon) and also those who followed them exactly (in faith). Allaah is well-pleased with them as they are well-pleased with Him. He has prepared for them Gardens under which rivers flow (Paradise), to dwell therein forever. That is the supreme success.**⟩—(*Surah Al-Tawbah:100)*

So Allaah, the Most Exalted, the Most Magnificent, has included and described them as those who follow Muhaajiroon and the Ansaar, upon a condition, "**who followed them exactly (in faith).**" *Meaning truly followed them with precision and integrity, not merely putting forth a claim or outwardly attributing or attaching themselves to them without actually realizing their guidance. This is true whether that shortfall is caused by ignorance or by the following of desires. Not everyone who attributes himself to the first three generations is true in his assertion unless he follows them precisely and with integrity. This is in fact a condition, a condition placed by Allaah, the Most Glorified and the Most Exalted. The wording* "**exactly (in faith).** *meaning precisely, with integrity, as well as entirely.*

What is required in truly following them is that you study the methodology of the Salaf, that you understand it, and that you are firmly attached to it. But as for individuals who simply attribute themselves to them, while they do not really understand their methodology nor their way, then this does not really benefit them with anything, and does not actually help them in anyway. Such people are not from those upon the way of the Salaf and should not be considered Salafees. Because they are not following the first generations precisely with integrity, as indeed Allaah, the Most Glorified and the Most Exalted, has placed this as the condition for their following of them to be true.

....The one who proceeds upon the methodology of the Salaf must have two characteristics, as we have previously mentioned. Firstly, actually understanding the methodology of the first generations, and the second matter is adhering firmly to it, even when it causes him hardship and discomfort. As he will certainly encounter a great deal of that from those who oppose this path of guidance. He will encounter harassment. He will encounter stubbornness. He will encounter false accusations. He will face having directed towards him evil names and false labels. However, he must remain patient in the face of this, as he is convinced and satisfied with what he stands upon. He should be not shaken or troubled in the face of a whirlwind of difficulties. He should not be affected or changed by what he encounters of different trials, but remains patient when facing them until he meets his Lord.

Accordingly, one must firstly learn the methodology of the first three generation, and then follow it exactly with integrity, while being patient with what you encounter from the people due to this adherence. Yet this in and of itself is also not enough, it is additionally necessary to spread the methodology of the first generations. It is required to invite the people to Allaah and invite them to the way of the Salaf, to explain it to the people and spread this way among them. The one who does this is Salafee in reality and truth. But as for the one who claims Salafeeyah, yet he does not truly understand the methodology of the Salaf, or he does indeed understand it yet fails to truly follow it, but simply follows what the people are upon, or merely follows what happens to agree with his desires. This one is not Salafee, even if he calls and labels himself that.

This fact demands from us that we place great importance in fully comprehending the way of the first generations and studying their methodology in beliefs, character, and actions in every environment and situation. As the path and methodology of the first three generations is that methodology upon which the Messenger of Allaah, may the praise and salutations be upon him, was upon, and is that way which those who follow the best of generations and walk upon their path, will proceed upon until the Final Hour is established....

...As such, it is required that the one who claims this way, or connects himself to the Salaf make this descriptive name a reality and make his attachment to them something which truly reflects the way of the first generations in beliefs, and in statements, and in actions, and in general dealings. So that he may be a true Salafee and that he may be a righteous example to others and someone who sincerely reflects the way of the righteous first generations of Islaam." [1]

We ask Allaah for success in each of our efforts to both learn and reflect the clear path of the first three generations, in every area of our individual lives, the lives of our spouses, and the lives of our children. And the success is from Allaah.

---

[1]   From the lecture "Salafeeyah, Its Reality And Its Characteristics" http://www.alfawzan.af.org.sa/

30 Days of Guidance: Learning Fundamental Principles of Islaam

A Short Journey Within the Work al-Ibaanah al-Sughrah With Sheikh ʿAbdul-ʿAzeez Ibn ʿAbdullah ar-Raajhee

[Exercise Workbook]

Compiled and Translated by:
Abu Sukhailah Khalil Ibn-Abelahyi

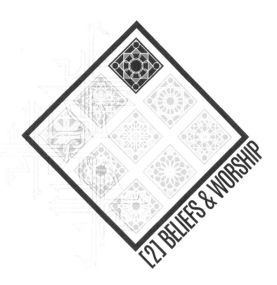

[2] BELIEFS & WORSHIP

How to use this Exercise Workbook

This workbook can be used to make it simpler for the one administering a study circle to check all exercise homewor from the answer key which is available at the back of the [Self-Study / Teachers Edition].The exercise workbooks can be collected after class or at another convenient time for student work to be checked before proceeding to the next day.

A small marking area has been added for indicating correct and incorrect answers at the bottom of each page. Depending on question type , there is a [/ 1] or [/ 3] for recording the number of correct answers out of total answers on that specific page. Partial scores can be given for essay answers that may not completely fulfill the needed answer, and then clarifying notes added in the teacher notes section below the same essay answer area. In addition, there is also an final total correct area i.e. =[/ 15] at the end of each day's section for recording the total number of correct answers for each individual day's exercises.

SCORING EACH DAYS EXERCISE ASSESSMENT TOTAL

Multiply the total points of correct answers (max. 15) times (X) 6.7 for score out of 100.

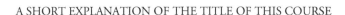

Sheikh Muhammad Ibn Saaleh al-'Utheimeen, may Allaah have mercy upon him, said,

"Allaah the Most High's Sharee'ah, is likely to be attacked, from the time that it emerged from Makkah until this very day. Indeed the Sharee'ah of Allaah is something which is regularly, or often, attacked.

Just as Allaah, the Most High says, ❖ ***Thus have We made for every Prophet an enemy among the disbelievers, polytheists, and criminals.*** ❖-(Surah Al-Furqaan: 31).

Certainly every prophet had enemies, and everyone who followed one of the prophets who was sent, would likewise have enemies. This is something which is necessary, as it is the sunnah of Allaah, the Most Glorified and the Most Exalted. The true path is not a smooth path with no obstacles, surrounded by only flowers and blossoms. Rather the true path of Allaah is hard and difficult.

It is necessary that Allaah, the Most Glorified and the Most Exalted, according to a wisdom that is with Him, places those who would oppose the truth in order that the truth be known, and in order that it become something which manifests as something clear and dominant over falsehood.

Additionally, this is in order that Allaah would make clear who are those individuals who strive in His path, and those who proceed patiently upon His guidance."

(From his well-known series -Open Door Gatherings 3/66. may Allaah have abundant mercy upon him)

TABLE OF CONTENTS

TEST YOUR UNDERSTANDING:

3 min

TRUE & FALSE QUESTIONS

[Circle the correct letter for each individual sentence from today's content.]

01. The main thing to consider when doing something is to make [T / F] sure you have a good intention.

02. It is important to ask Allaah to guide us to every matter that [T / F] will make us successful as a Muslim.

03. It is permissible to do acts of worship in a unique and new way [T / F] as long as you are sincere and doing so purely for Allaah's sake.

6 min

FILL IN THE BLANK QUESTIONS

[Enter the correct individual words to complete the sentences from today's content.]

04. Outward success is found if we are_____ in our statements and we put forward _____ actions.

05. If our deeds are lacking in _____ then this is a type of associating others with _____ .

06. If our deeds are lacking in adherence to the Sunnah and we follow a new method of worshiping, then this is a type of _____ in the religion.

7-12 min

INTERACTIVE QUESTIONS & EXERCISES

COMPREHENSIVE UNDERSTANDING QUESTIONS

07. Why is it important for someone to seek Allaah's assistance in both adhering to the Sunnah and having sincerity of intention for Allaah alone, and not just one?

TEACHER NOTES / CORRECTIONS

✳[/ 3]

7-12 min

08. Give examples of three invalid intentions which a person may intend in his heart when doing an outwardly good action.

_____

_____

_____

_____

_____

_____

_____

_____

_____

_____

_____

_____

_____

_____

_____

_____

_____

_____

_____

_____

_____

_____

_____

_____

_____

_____

_____

_____

TEACHER NOTES / CORRECTIONS

_____

_____

_____

_____

_____

09. Give examples of three acts of worship which are done by Muslims sincerely, but which go against the revealed guidance of the Sharee'ah.

TEACHER NOTES / CORRECTIONS

✳[/3]=[/15]

TEST YOUR UNDERSTANDING:

TRUE & FALSE QUESTIONS

[Circle the correct letter for each individual sentence from today's content.]

3 min

01. The previous prophets did not know about the coming of the   [T / F]
     Prophet Muhammad.

02. All the previous revealed guidance of Allaah has been completed   [T / F]
     in the guidance given to the Prophet Mohammed.

03. The righteous Muslims, as worshipers of Allaah, are all equal   [T / F]
     in rank and merit.

FILL IN THE BLANK QUESTIONS

[Enter the correct individual words to complete the sentences from today's content.]

6 min

04. Every previous prophet had a _____ with Allaah about the coming
     of the prophet Muhammad.

05. The prophet _____ will descend in the later times and judge
     according to the _____ .

06. _____ was the best of those within the Muslim Ummah who
     was not a _____ .

COMPREHENSIVE UNDERSTANDING QUESTIONS

07. What is a possible benefit of knowing the different ranks and positions of excellence of those who are part of the Muslim Ummah?

TEACHER NOTES / CORRECTIONS

✳[/3]

7-12min

08. Why is it important to understand that Islaam completes and abrogates the guidance given to the previous prophets and messengers?

_____
_____
_____
_____
_____
_____
_____
_____
_____
_____
_____
_____
_____
_____
_____
_____
_____
_____
_____
_____
_____
_____
_____
_____
_____
_____

TEACHER NOTES / CORRECTIONS

_____
_____
_____
_____
_____
_____

09. Mention any two matters that the Muslims have agreed upon by consensus.

TEACHER NOTES / CORRECTIONS

TEST YOUR UNDERSTANDING:

TRUE & FALSE QUESTIONS

[Circle the correct letter for each individual sentence from today's content.]

3 min

01. It is permissible to follow any path or religion as long as your [T / F] intention is to please Allaah.

02. Just as there are many ways of misguidance, there are many [T / F] paths upon the truth and guidance.

03. Each path of misguidance has a Shaytaan inviting to it and [T / F] making it appealing to people.

FILL IN THE BLANK QUESTIONS

[Enter the correct individual words to complete the sentences from today's content.]

6 min

04. There is a single _____ path and many paths of _____ .

05. Every path of misguidance has a _____ upon it _____ people to it.

06. Both _____ and _____ are part of the paths of misguidance.

COMPREHENSIVE UNDERSTANDING QUESTIONS

7-12 min

07. What command and what prohibition is found within the mentioned verse in Surah Al-An'am? Give a practical everyday example of how someone may properly follow the command, and properly adhere to the prohibition mentioned.

TEACHER NOTES / CORRECTIONS

✱[/ 3]

08.　Name two paths of misguidance and briefly describe why some people might believe that they are good to follow.

_____

_____

_____

_____

_____

_____

_____

_____

_____

_____

_____

_____

_____

_____

_____

_____

_____

_____

_____

_____

_____

_____

_____

_____

TEACHER NOTES / CORRECTIONS

_____

_____

_____

_____

_____

09. What are two possible important means of helping a Muslim understand what the straight path is, and proceed steadfastly upon it.

_____

_____

_____

_____

_____

_____

_____

_____

_____

_____

_____

_____

_____

_____

_____

_____

_____

_____

_____

_____

_____

_____

_____

_____

TEACHER NOTES / CORRECTIONS

_____

_____

_____

_____

_____

*[/ 3] = [/15]

DAY - 04

TEST YOUR UNDERSTANDING:

TRUE & FALSE QUESTIONS

[Circle the correct letter for each individual sentence from today's content.]

3 min

01. There are many sects found within the history of the Muslim   [T / F]
     Ummah and they are all considered Muslims.

02. The scholars have identified and distinguished the various sects   [T / F]
     among the Muslims.

03. The saved sect is everyone who says they are Muslim, and   [T / F]
     claims their religion is Islaam.

FILL IN THE BLANK QUESTIONS

[Enter the correct individual words to complete the sentences from today's content.]

6 min

04. The seventy-two astray sects within the Ummah all have some form of
     _____.

05. Due to major disbelief the extremely deviant sects such as the _____
     , are considered _____ of the boundaries of Islaam.

06. The saved sect remains upon what the _____ and the
     _____ were upon originally.

COMPREHENSIVE UNDERSTANDING QUESTIONS

7-12 min

DAY - 04

07.   Name three sects or groups who are misguided and upon innovation but remain within the Muslim Ummah.

TEACHER NOTES / CORRECTIONS

*[/3]

08. Name two sects or groups whose extreme misguidance takes them outside the boundaries of the Muslim Ummah.

_____

_____

_____

_____

_____

_____

_____

_____

_____

_____

_____

_____

_____

_____

_____

_____

_____

_____

_____

_____

_____

_____

_____

_____

_____

_____

_____

_____

_____

TEACHER NOTES / CORRECTIONS

_____

_____

_____

_____

_____

09. What are two essential characteristics that distinguish Muslims from the saved sect as compared to the astray sects?

TEACHER NOTES / CORRECTIONS

*[/3]=[/15]

TEST YOUR UNDERSTANDING:

TRUE & FALSE QUESTIONS

[Circle the correct letter for each individual sentence from today's content.]

3 min

01. Allaah supports and is pleased with anyone who calls themselves   [T / F]
Muslim.

02. The foundation of the saved sect are the Companions of the   [T / F]
Messenger of Allaah.

03. People's deviations away from guidance will not lead them to   [T / F]
the Hellfire if they are sincere.

FILL IN THE BLANK QUESTIONS

[Enter the correct individual words to complete the sentences from today's content.]

6 min

04. The truth is what is found the Book of _____ and in adherence
to the _____ .

05. It is an _____ to adhere to the _____ of the Companions
of the Messenger of Allaah.

06. _____ as well as doubts and _____ are all considered
deviations away from the Sunnah.

COMPREHENSIVE UNDERSTANDING QUESTIONS

7-12 min

DAY - 05

07. Give an example of one sect or group who has separated from the Jamaa'ah and one belief they have innovated.

_____

_____

_____

_____

_____

_____

_____

_____

_____

_____

_____

_____

_____

_____

_____

_____

_____

_____

_____

_____

_____

_____

TEACHER NOTES / CORRECTIONS

_____

_____

_____

_____

_____

✳[/ 3]

7-12min

08. Give an separate example of another sect or group who has separated from the Jamaa'ah and one practice they have innovated.

_____
_____
_____
_____
_____
_____
_____
_____
_____
_____
_____
_____
_____
_____
_____
_____
_____
_____
_____
_____
_____
_____
_____
_____
_____
_____
_____

TEACHER NOTES / CORRECTIONS

_____
_____
_____
_____
_____

09. Is it possible to be part of the Jamaa'ah united upon the truth, but not follow the way of the Companions? Explain your answer.

TEACHER NOTES / CORRECTIONS

*[/3]=[/15]

TEST YOUR UNDERSTANDING:

TRUE & FALSE QUESTIONS

[Circle the correct letter for each individual sentence from today's content.]

01. It is not an obligation to hold fast onto the rope of Allaah.   [T / F]

02. The issue of sticking close to the Jamaa'ah, involves both a   [T / F] command and the prohibition.

03. We can hold fast to the Rope of Allaah, by simply following   [T / F] only the guidance of the Qur'aan.

FILL IN THE BLANK QUESTIONS

[Enter the correct individual words to complete the sentences from today's content.]

04. The revealed source texts _____ separating into different groups and _____ .

05. Allaah's religion is what He sent down within His _____ , and upon the tongue of His _____ .

06. _____ and _____ can result from failing to act upon revealed guidance.

COMPREHENSIVE UNDERSTANDING QUESTIONS

7-12 min

DAY - 06

07. What are two of the characteristics of the Jamaa'ah of the Muslims upon the truth in any age?

_____

_____

_____

_____

_____

_____

_____

_____

_____

_____

_____

_____

_____

_____

_____

_____

_____

_____

_____

_____

_____

_____

TEACHER NOTES / CORRECTIONS

_____

_____

_____

_____

*[/ 3]

7-12 min

08.   Give a practical example of how holding on to the Rope of Allaah establishes unity among Muslims?

_____
_____
_____
_____
_____
_____
_____
_____
_____
_____
_____
_____
_____
_____
_____
_____
_____
_____
_____
_____
_____
_____
_____
_____

TEACHER NOTES / CORRECTIONS

_____
_____
_____
_____
_____

09. What is something that leads to the hearts of the Muslims being united? What is a specific benefit of this in regard to the position of the Muslim Ummah in the world?

TEACHER NOTES / CORRECTIONS

*[/3]=[/15]

TEST YOUR UNDERSTANDING:

3 min

TRUE & FALSE QUESTIONS

[Circle the correct letter for each individual sentence from today's content.]

01. Those known as Shee'ah have several different levels of   [T / F] misguidance.

02. A Muslim should declare himself free from every misguided   [T / F] sect.

03. Some extreme Shee'ah believe that Allaah embodied Himself   [T / F] in the form of 'Alee.

6 min

FILL IN THE BLANK QUESTIONS

[Enter the correct individual words to complete the sentences from today's content.]

04. Zayd Ibn 'Alee Ibn Husain spoke well of and _____ for Allaah to have mercy upon Abu _____ and ' _____ .

05. Some Shee'ah believe that the angel Jibreel made a mistake bringing the revelation to the _____ _____ , as they falsely claim that Jibreel was sent to bring revelation to ' _____ .

06. A Muslim should oppose the incorrect _____ and separate from the _____ upon any new name which opposes the guidance of the _____ .

COMPREHENSIVE UNDERSTANDING QUESTIONS

7-12 min

07. Name two countries where many people adhere to the misguided sect of the Shee'ah.

DAY - 07

_____

_____

_____

_____

_____

_____

_____

_____

_____

_____

_____

_____

_____

_____

_____

_____

_____

_____

_____

_____

_____

_____

TEACHER NOTES / CORRECTIONS

_____

_____

_____

_____

_____

✷[/3]

7-12 min

08. Name someone who opposed the false beliefs of the Raafidhah? Also discuss one of their false beliefs held by some of them connected to the Book of Allaah, the Qur'aan.

_____

_____

_____

_____

_____

_____

_____

_____

_____

_____

_____

_____

_____

_____

_____

_____

_____

_____

_____

_____

_____

_____

_____

_____

_____

_____

_____

TEACHER NOTES / CORRECTIONS

_____

_____

_____

_____

_____

_____

09. Who initially opposed the false beliefs of the sect of the Khawaarij? Also mention one of their well known false beliefs.

7-12 min

TEACHER NOTES / CORRECTIONS

*[/ 3] = [/15]

TEST YOUR UNDERSTANDING:

3min

TRUE & FALSE QUESTIONS

[Circle the correct letter for each individual sentence from today's content.]

01. The strangeness of Islaam is something negative. [T / F]
02. Islaam will never be strange again since it is all over the world. [T / F]
03. The Prophet praised the strangers who held firmly to revealed [T / F] guidance.

6min

FILL IN THE BLANK QUESTIONS

[Enter the correct individual words to complete the sentences from today's content.]

04. Islaam _____ as something strange in the city of _____ .

05. Islaam spread significantly in the _____ year when the Arab tribes and _____ came to _____ .

06. _____ and the rewards of _____ are promised to the ones who are strangers upon _____ .

COMPREHENSIVE UNDERSTANDING QUESTIONS

7-12 min

DAY - 08

07.   Describe three ways in which Islaam is considered strange in our time and age.

_____

_____

_____

_____

_____

_____

_____

_____

_____

_____

_____

_____

_____

_____

_____

_____

_____

_____

_____

_____

_____

_____

TEACHER NOTES / CORRECTIONS

_____

_____

_____

_____

✴[/ 3]

08. Explain two characteristics of the strangers by giving a possible practical example for each of those characteristics.

TEACHER NOTES / CORRECTIONS

09. Can Islaam only be strange among non-Muslims or also possibly amongst the Muslims? Briefly explain your answer giving examples if necessary.

TEACHER NOTES / CORRECTIONS

✲[/ 3] = [/15]

TEST YOUR UNDERSTANDING:

TRUE & FALSE QUESTIONS

[Circle the correct letter for each individual sentence from today's content.]

01. The Companions of the Messenger of Allaah differed in some matters. [T / F]

02. It is wrong to blindly follow a scholar in every single thing they say. [T / F]

3 min

03. We can understand what is the truth simply by looking at someone who practices it. [T / F]

FILL IN THE BLANK QUESTIONS

[Enter the correct individual words to complete the sentences from today's content.]

04. In the dispute about the _____ the majority of the Companions of the Messenger of Allaah stood with _____ .

05. The scholars receive one _____ for their _____ to reach the correct conclusion, and a second _____ due to actually being _____ .

6 min

06. We always have an _____ to hold firmly to the _____ and the _____ .

COMPREHENSIVE UNDERSTANDING QUESTIONS

7-12 min

07. Give an example of a matter of fiqh or implementation of the source texts in which you know some of our modern-day scholars differ with one another?

DAY - 09

TEACHER NOTES / CORRECTIONS

*[/3]

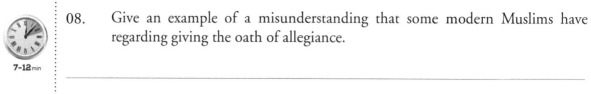

7-12 min

08. Give an example of a misunderstanding that some modern Muslims have regarding giving the oath of allegiance.

DAY - 09

TEACHER NOTES / CORRECTIONS

09. Try to explain one reason that the position of Ibn 'Abbaas in supporting 'Alee, was actually following the Messenger of Allaah, and not biased partisanship towards 'Alee.

_____

TEACHER NOTES / CORRECTIONS

_____

*[/3]=[/15]

TEST YOUR UNDERSTANDING:

TRUE & FALSE QUESTIONS

[Circle the correct letter for each individual sentence from today's content.]

01. The angel Jibreel brought two types of revelation to the [T / F] Messenger of Allaah.

02. Some hadeeth narrations contain statements from Allaah. [T / F]

03. The Qur'aan is the only knowledge the Prophet of Allaah [T / F] possessed.

FILL IN THE BLANK QUESTIONS

[Enter the correct individual words to complete the sentences from today's content.]

04. _____ used to teach the prophet the _____ just as he used to teach him the Qur'aan.

05. The Prophet himself, said to us, {Indeed I've been _____ the _____ and that which is _____ it.}

06. Qur'aan itself is from the _____ of Allaah in both _____ and _____ .

COMPREHENSIVE UNDERSTANDING QUESTIONS

7-12 min

07. Is it required that we accept all the knowledge which the Messenger of Allaah came with, or just the Qur'aan?

DAY - 10

TEACHER NOTES / CORRECTIONS

✳[/ 3]

08. Describe one of the authentic ways the text of the Qur'aan is used in a form of worship.

DAY - 10

_____
_____
_____
_____
_____
_____
_____
_____
_____
_____
_____
_____
_____
_____
_____
_____
_____
_____
_____
_____
_____
_____
_____
_____
_____
_____
_____

TEACHER NOTES / CORRECTIONS

_____
_____
_____
_____
_____
_____

09. What verse indicates to us that all religious statements of the Prophet are a form of revelation? How does it clarify the false claim that he made up parts of Islaam?

TEACHER NOTES / CORRECTIONS

*[/ 3]=[/15]

TEST YOUR UNDERSTANDING:

TRUE & FALSE QUESTIONS

[Circle the correct letter for each individual sentence from today's content.]

3min

DAY - 11

01. Many commands of the Qur'aan are general without specifics and details. [T / F]

02. The Sunnah clarifies the commands of the Qur'aan, but does not bring any new commands. [T / F]

03. A person can take what he wants from the Sunnah but must accept the entire Qur'aan. [T / F]

FILL IN THE BLANK QUESTIONS

[Enter the correct individual words to complete the sentences from today's content.]

6min

04. The person who rejects and turns away from the Sunnah _____ off his _____ to Allaah.

05. Not every matter of _____ is detailed in the _____ .

06. The Messenger of Allaah was given the _____ and that which is like it, meaning the_____.

COMPREHENSIVE UNDERSTANDING QUESTIONS

7-12 min

07. Give another example, other than those mentioned, of a command in Islaam in which the details are found in the Sunnah, not all in the Qur'aan.

DAY - 11

TEACHER NOTES / CORRECTIONS

✳[/3]

08. Is it possible to follow the command in the Qur'aan to obey the Messenger while rejecting the Sunnah? Give an example to explain your answer.

TEACHER NOTES / CORRECTIONS

09. Give authentic examples of one command, and one prohibition coming from the Messenger of Allaah, which are not found in the Qur'aan.

TEACHER NOTES / CORRECTIONS

TEST YOUR UNDERSTANDING:

TRUE & FALSE QUESTIONS

[Circle the correct letter for each individual sentence from today's content.]

3min

01. Knowledge in Islaam is generally carried by the scholars. [T / F]
02. Those who are ignorant only cause harm to themselves and not others. [T / F]
03. Beneficial knowledge is something specific to the affairs of our religion. [T / F]

FILL IN THE BLANK QUESTIONS

[Enter the correct individual words to complete the sentences from today's content.]

04. The one who adheres firmly to the Sunnah is _____ in this world from entering into _____ and _____ , and in the life to come saved from entering _____.
05. Giving life to knowledge makes both one's _____ and _____ life steadfast and firm.
06. The noble guiding scholars _____ against _____ in the religion and the people of _____ .

COMPREHENSIVE UNDERSTANDING QUESTIONS

7-12 min

07. Give examples of two guiding scholars who were upon the Sunnah who died in this age or modern period.

DAY - 12

TEACHER NOTES / CORRECTIONS

✳[/ 3]

08. Give examples of two ignorant modern individuals who people wrongly consider scholars, and who misguide others.

TEACHER NOTES / CORRECTIONS

09. Give two examples of incorrect rulings that you generally heard about coming from ignorant individuals which only increase the Muslims in misguidance and harm.

TEACHER NOTES / CORRECTIONS

*[/3]=[/15]

TEST YOUR UNDERSTANDING:

TRUE & FALSE QUESTIONS

[Circle the correct letter for each individual sentence from today's content.]

3 min

01. There is a greater reward for adhering to the truth during times [T / F] of difficulty.

02. The one who gains the reward of fifty of the Companions has [T / F] excelled them in merit.

03. None of the prophets and messengers have distinct merits. [T / F]

FILL IN THE BLANK QUESTIONS

[Enter the correct individual words to complete the sentences from today's content.]

6 min

04. The _____ of the Messenger of Allaah have several distinctive _____ .

05. Those who hold firmly to the _____ in the _____ ages will not find those to _____ them.

06. The Muslim who holds firmly to the _____ is far away from _____ .

COMPREHENSIVE UNDERSTANDING QUESTIONS

7-12 min

07.   Discuss two mentioned distinctive merits of the Companions, and explain why no one shares these merits with them.

DAY - 13

```
TEACHER NOTES / CORRECTIONS
```

✳[/ 3]

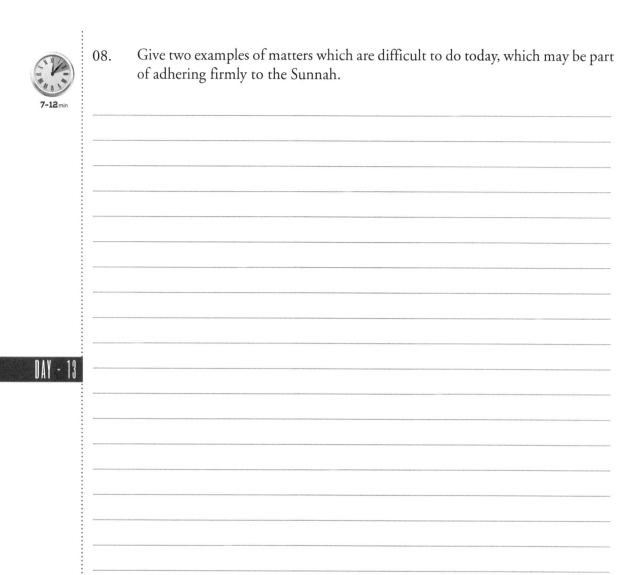

7-12 min

08. Give two examples of matters which are difficult to do today, which may be part of adhering firmly to the Sunnah.

TEACHER NOTES / CORRECTIONS

09. Give two possible examples of beneficial practices or deeds that might be considered from those in which it is hard to find other Muslims to assist them in doing.

TEACHER NOTES / CORRECTIONS

*[/3]=[/15]

TEST YOUR UNDERSTANDING:

TRUE & FALSE QUESTIONS

[Circle the correct letter for each individual sentence from today's content.]

3min

01. The Hajj pilgrimage must only be performed completely [T / F] separately from 'Umrah.

02. It is only important that we adhere to the Qur'aan and Sunnah [T / F] the Prophet and nothing else.

03. A statement from one of the rightly guided khalifahs can be [T / F] followed instead of an authentic affirmed Sunnah.

FILL IN THE BLANK QUESTIONS

[Enter the correct individual words to complete the sentences from today's content.]

6min

04. Before the coming of Islaam, tamattu' was something _____ within the months of _____ .

05. The sunnah of the rightly guided _____ is taken and _____ whenever there is no guidance within the _____ _____ about a specific issue or matter.

06. The additional _____ on the day of _____ , when necessary, is considered from the _____ of a rightly guided khalifah.

DAY - 14

COMPREHENSIVE UNDERSTANDING QUESTIONS

7-12 min

07.   Give an example of a practice of the Sunnah that might be considered strange to some of the Muslims today.

DAY - 14

TEACHER NOTES / CORRECTIONS

*[/ 3]

08. Is it possible that a statement of one of the rightly guided khalifahs might be incorrect? Explain your answer.

_____

_____

_____

_____

_____

_____

_____

_____

_____

_____

_____

_____

_____

DAY - 14

_____

_____

_____

_____

_____

_____

_____

_____

_____

_____

_____

_____

_____

_____

TEACHER NOTES / CORRECTIONS

_____

_____

_____

_____

_____

09. Explain why Ibn 'Abbaas was upset with those Muslims who were following the position of some of the rightly guided khalifahs?

TEACHER NOTES / CORRECTIONS

*[/3]=[/15]

TEST YOUR UNDERSTANDING:

TRUE & FALSE QUESTIONS

[Circle the correct letter for each individual sentence from today's content.]

3min

01. The Companions of the Messenger of Allaah all have the same   [T / F] rank.

02. Some of the events during the life of the Prophet led to many   [T / F] people embracing Islaam.

03. The treaty of al-Hudaybeeyah did not affect the spread of   [T / F] Islaam.

DAY - 15

FILL IN THE BLANK QUESTIONS

[Enter the correct individual words to complete the sentences from today's content.]

6min

04. The first Muslims to embrace Islaam were the _____ , who migrated from _____ to _____

05. The treaty of al-Hudaybeeyah is called an _____ and _____ for Islaam, and the Muslims.

06. The people of Mecca, or their allies, _____ the treaty of al-Hudaybeeyah after _____ years.

COMPREHENSIVE UNDERSTANDING QUESTIONS

7-12 min

07.   Give examples of two difficulties which the Muhaajiroon faced that those who embraced Islaam later did not encounter.

DAY - 15

TEACHER NOTES / CORRECTIONS

✳[/ 3]

08. How was the period right after the treaty of al-Hudaybeeyah different in terms of spreading Islaam to the people?

_____
_____
_____
_____
_____
_____
_____
_____
_____
_____
_____
_____
_____
_____
_____

DAY - 15

_____
_____
_____
_____
_____
_____
_____
_____
_____
_____

TEACHER NOTES / CORRECTIONS

_____
_____
_____
_____
_____

09. Name another well-known Companion from the Muhaajiroon, and describe one way that they helped support Islaam.

TEACHER NOTES / CORRECTIONS

*[/3]=[/15]

TEST YOUR UNDERSTANDING:

TRUE & FALSE QUESTIONS

[Circle the correct letter for each individual sentence from today's content.]

3min

01. There is no difference in learning from books or from scholars   [T / F]
    directly.

02. There will come a time in which knowledge will disappear and   [T / F]
    not be easily found among people.

03. It is possible for anyone to issue correct rulings and judgments   [T / F]
    in Islaam.

DAY - 16

FILL IN THE BLANK QUESTIONS

[Enter the correct individual words to complete the sentences from today's content.]

6min

04. Allaah does not take away the _____ by taking it away from
    the _____ of the people.

05. The _____ are needed to be those who _____ matters
    to the people and _____ the intended meanings of the Qur'aan
    and Sunnah.

06. The people of _____ wrongly throw one source text against
    another so that they clash or _____ .

COMPREHENSIVE UNDERSTANDING QUESTIONS

7-12 min

07. Explain misconceptions or ideas that people hold that cause them to refrain from learning from scholars.

_____

_____

_____

_____

_____

_____

_____

_____

_____

_____

_____

_____

DAY - 16

_____

_____

_____

_____

_____

_____

_____

_____

TEACHER NOTES / CORRECTIONS

_____

_____

_____

_____

∗[/3]

08. Give the name of one well-known scholar of this age who has died, and mention one of the areas of knowledge which they were proficient in.

TEACHER NOTES / CORRECTIONS

09. Discuss one shortcoming of studying only from books and not from the scholars themselves. Give a possible example to explain your answer.

TEACHER NOTES / CORRECTIONS

*[/ 3] = [/15]

TEST YOUR UNDERSTANDING:

TRUE & FALSE QUESTIONS

[Circle the correct letter for each individual sentence from today's content.]

3 min

01. The people of misguidance oppose the guidance of the Sunnah [T / F] in several ways.

02. It is not important to carefully select the books one reads, as [T / F] long as they are from Muslims.

03. People are often confused as to who are actually reliable scholars [T / F] we should benefit from.

FILL IN THE BLANK QUESTIONS

[Enter the correct individual words to complete the sentences from today's content.]

DAY - 17

6 min

04. A _____ person who does not possess a significant amount of _____ can be misled by _____ .

05. Jahm Ibn Safwaan is the originator of the sect of the _____ .

06. The subtle_____ in the books of the people of falsehood may not be recognized by the _____ of people who read them.

[/6]*

COMPREHENSIVE UNDERSTANDING QUESTIONS

7-12 min

07. Give one way the people are misled by those using modern technology, causing them to wrongly believe that someone is a reliable scholar.

_____

_____

_____

_____

_____

_____

_____

_____

_____

_____

_____

_____

_____

DAY - 17

_____

_____

_____

_____

_____

_____

_____

TEACHER NOTES / CORRECTIONS

_____

_____

_____

_____

✱[/ 3]

08. Explain one way a general Muslim can be truly confident that a book they want to benefit from is sound and acceptable.

TEACHER NOTES / CORRECTIONS

09. Name one of the leaders or ideological figureheads from any one of the misguided movements or groups present among the Muslims today.

DAY - 17

TEACHER NOTES / CORRECTIONS

*[/3]=[/15]

TEST YOUR UNDERSTANDING:

TRUE & FALSE QUESTIONS

[Circle the correct letter for each individual sentence from today's content.]

3 min

01. It acceptable to sit and listen to people mock Islaam, as long as [T / F] you don't join in.

02. The person who sits in a gathering of wrongdoing must speak [T / F] up to stop them or leave.

03. Muslims have been prohibited from taking non-Muslims as [T / F] close friends.

FILL IN THE BLANK QUESTIONS

[Enter the correct individual words to complete the sentences from today's content.]

6 min

04. The believers have been ordered to _____ from those who _____ against their clear religion.

05. It is allowed to _____ non-Muslims in order to _____ them to Islaam, just as the Prophet did.

06. If a Muslim is _____ with that sin and transgression that people are doing in a _____ where there is wrongdoing, he is considered like one of those _____ .

[/ 6]*

COMPREHENSIVE UNDERSTANDING QUESTIONS

7-12 min

07.	Give an example in which a Muslim might find themselves in one of the situations mentioned. What is a good way to implement the guidelines mentioned?

_____

_____

_____

_____

_____

_____

_____

_____

_____

_____

_____

_____

DAY - 18

_____

_____

_____

_____

_____

_____

TEACHER NOTES / CORRECTIONS

_____

_____

_____

_____

✳[/ 3]

08. Briefly explain how speaking up when falsehood is mentioned benefits you.

DAY - 18

TEACHER NOTES / CORRECTIONS

09. What is one of the dangers of taking non-Muslims as close friends related to this discussion?

TEACHER NOTES / CORRECTIONS

*[/3]=[/15]

TEST YOUR UNDERSTANDING:

TRUE & FALSE QUESTIONS

[Circle the correct letter for each individual sentence from today's content.]

3 min

01. People's desires generally guide them to that which is good for them.   [T / F]

02. It is important to follow the truth no matter what our desires call us to.   [T / F]

03. What is considered obedience to Allaah is different for every person.   [T / F]

FILL IN THE BLANK QUESTIONS

[Enter the correct individual words to complete the sentences from today's content.]

6 min

DAY - 19

04. Our _____ are often something which _____ and are a _____ to accepting the truth.

05. Steadfastness means to hold _____ to the _____ and the _____ .

06. We should _____ what comes within the _____ source texts, not our _____ .

COMPREHENSIVE UNDERSTANDING QUESTIONS

7-12min

07. What might be one cause of someone wrongly believing that our desires are something pleasing to Allaah?

DAY - 19

TEACHER NOTES / CORRECTIONS

✳[/ 3]

08. Give a practical example of how someone's desires might prevent them from accepting something required in Islaam. Write out their possible false excuse.

TEACHER NOTES / CORRECTIONS

09. Give a practical example of an issue a Muslim might need to be steadfast in, specifically in our modern age and time.

TEACHER NOTES / CORRECTIONS

*[/ 3] = [/15]

TEST YOUR UNDERSTANDING:

TRUE & FALSE QUESTIONS

[Circle the correct letter for each individual sentence from today's content.]

3 min

01. It is acceptable for a Muslim to choose between his opinion and   [T / F]
what is found in the Sunnah.

02. Speaking from your opinions in relation to the religion is   [T / F]
something blameworthy.

03. The Muslims upon guidance place the knowledge of the   [T / F]
Sunnah above their opinions and perceptions.

FILL IN THE BLANK QUESTIONS

[Enter the correct individual words to complete the sentences from today's content.]

6 min

DAY - 20

04. The people of opinions who follow their _____ , are

_____ and opponents of the authentic _____ of the
Prophet.

05. The people who are infatuated with their own perceptions and opinions,
break free of the guidance of the _____ from the _____ .

06. Beneficial narrations are brought to us so we can understand, try to

_____ , and _____ upon them.

COMPREHENSIVE UNDERSTANDING QUESTIONS

7-12 min

07. Give an example of a common opinion or perception found among non-Muslims that goes against the guidance of Islaam.

DAY - 20

TEACHER NOTES / CORRECTIONS

✳[/ 3]

08. Give an example of a common opinion or perception found among Muslims today that goes against the guidance of Islaam.

_____

_____

_____

_____

_____

_____

_____

_____

_____

_____

_____

_____

_____

_____

_____

_____

_____

_____

_____

_____

_____

_____

DAY - 20

_____

_____

_____

TEACHER NOTES / CORRECTIONS

_____

_____

_____

_____

_____

[/ 3]*

09. Explain one false reason an ignorant Muslim might use to justify placing his opinion over and above the clear guidance of Islaam.

_____

_____

_____

_____

_____

_____

_____

_____

_____

_____

_____

_____

_____

_____

_____

_____

_____

_____

_____

_____

DAY - 20

TEACHER NOTES / CORRECTIONS

_____

_____

_____

_____

_____

*[/ 3] = [/15]

TEST YOUR UNDERSTANDING:

TRUE & FALSE QUESTIONS

[Circle the correct letter for each individual sentence from today's content.]

3 min

01. If we are strong in our faith then there is no harm in debating [T / F] people.

02. There is more than one type of danger involved in sitting with [T / F] the people of misguidance.

03. The revealed guidance of Islaam is always superior to human [T / F] arguments and concepts.

FILL IN THE BLANK QUESTIONS

[Enter the correct individual words to complete the sentences from today's content.]

6 min

DAY - 21

04. The Sunnah is the _____ source of _____ .

05. The practice of _____ and argumentation produces _____ controversies, doubts, and _____ within Islaam.

06. Good company _____ you toward what is good, or turns you away from what is bad and _____, such as _____ in the religion.

COMPREHENSIVE UNDERSTANDING QUESTIONS

7-12 min

07. Give an example of a misconception, which the people who falsely claim to be engaged in Jihaad in our time, spread amongst the Muslims.

_____

_____

_____

_____

_____

_____

_____

_____

_____

_____

_____

_____

_____

_____

_____

_____

_____

_____

_____

_____

_____

_____

DAY - 21

TEACHER NOTES / CORRECTIONS

_____

_____

_____

_____

✳[/ 3]

08. Give an example of a misconception, which the people who claim to be engaged in efforts of calling to Allaah or da'wah in our time, spread amongst the Muslims.

TEACHER NOTES / CORRECTIONS

09. Give an example of a possible good response that a Muslim can give to someone who tries to get them to enter into an argument or debate.

DAY - 21

TEACHER NOTES / CORRECTIONS

*[/3]=[/15]

TEST YOUR UNDERSTANDING:

TRUE & FALSE QUESTIONS

[Circle the correct letter for each individual sentence from today's content.]

3min

01. A Muslim should listen to every argument and then decide [T / F]
     what is correct.
02. True knowledge in Islaam is based upon the foundation of [T / F]
     revealed guidance.
03. The early scholars of Islaam did not see any harm in personal [T / F]
     views and opinions.

FILL IN THE BLANK QUESTIONS

[Enter the correct individual words to complete the sentences from today's content.]

6min

04. Some scholars consider 'Umar Ibn 'Abdul-'Azeez, the _____ rightly
     guided _____ .
05. Someone who makes his _____ of Islaam the object of
     _____ and controversies will be _____ .
06. Controversies produce _____ and _____ within your
     understanding of _____ .

DAY - 22

COMPREHENSIVE UNDERSTANDING QUESTIONS

7-12 min

07. Give an example of a misconception related to the correct beliefs about Allaah which people often debate about.

_____

_____

_____

_____

_____

_____

_____

_____

_____

_____

_____

_____

_____

_____

_____

_____

_____

_____

_____

_____

DAY - 22

TEACHER NOTES / CORRECTIONS

_____

_____

_____

_____

✳[/3]

08. Give an example of a misconception related to women's dress which people often debate about.

TEACHER NOTES / CORRECTIONS

09. Give an example of a misconception about correcting mistakes which people often debate about.

DAY - 22

TEACHER NOTES / CORRECTIONS

*[/3]=[/15]

TEST YOUR UNDERSTANDING:

TRUE & FALSE QUESTIONS

[Circle the correct letter for each individual sentence from today's content.]

3 min

01. How someone starts out as a Muslim will not affect their   [T / F]
practice.
02. Muslims should strive to gain a foundation of sound knowledge   [T / F]
while they are young.
03. There have always been books which conveyed the correct   [T / F]
beliefs of Islaam since the first three generations of Muslims.

FILL IN THE BLANK QUESTIONS

[Enter the correct individual words to complete the sentences from today's content.]

6 min

04. If a Muslim is _____ upon the _____ the people of
the Sunnah and the Jamaa'ah he will generally _____ upon that.
05. The people of the Sunnah understand Allaah's_ _____ , upon the
of the first generations of _____ .
06. Allaah blessed Sheikh _____ Ibn 'Abdul-Wahaab, to
this revived _____ call.

DAY - 23

COMPREHENSIVE UNDERSTANDING QUESTIONS

7-12min

07. Give an example of something we can do to try to ensure that young Muslims today gain a sound understanding of Islaam when they are young.

_____

_____

_____

_____

_____

_____

_____

_____

_____

_____

_____

_____

_____

_____

_____

_____

_____

_____

_____

_____

_____

DAY - 23

TEACHER NOTES / CORRECTIONS

_____

_____

_____

_____

✱[/3]

08. What should a Muslim do if he encounters a conflict between the beliefs of a well-known scholar and the beliefs of the Companions?

_____

_____

_____

_____

_____

_____

_____

_____

_____

_____

_____

_____

_____

_____

_____

_____

_____

_____

_____

_____

_____

_____

_____

_____

_____

DAY - 23

TEACHER NOTES / CORRECTIONS

_____

_____

_____

_____

_____

_____

09. Describe one of the books of the beliefs of the people of the Sunnah which you have in your library, and write which scholar authored it.

_____

_____

_____

_____

_____

_____

_____

_____

_____

_____

_____

_____

_____

_____

_____

_____

_____

_____

_____

_____

_____

_____

_____

DAY - 23

TEACHER NOTES / CORRECTIONS

*[/3]=[/15]

TEST YOUR UNDERSTANDING:

TRUE & FALSE QUESTIONS

[Circle the correct letter for each individual sentence from today's content.]

3 min

01. We should have a strong love for our relatives, even when we see them disobeying Allaah. [T / F]

02. Our love for individuals does not have any connection to our love for Allaah and His Messenger. [T / F]

03. Loving someone for the sake of Allaah is different than loving them for a worldly reason. [T / F]

FILL IN THE BLANK QUESTIONS

[Enter the correct individual words to complete the sentences from today's content.]

6 min

04. A Muslim should love someone who _____ Allaah, even if they _____ with him in his _____ affairs.

05. You hate the one who commits _____ and _____ Allaah, even if he is someone _____ to you personally.

06. The scholars have warned us from _____ to those who generally speak from their own _____ and perceptions.

DAY - 24

[/6]＊

COMPREHENSIVE UNDERSTANDING QUESTIONS

7-12 min

07. Give a possible practical example of someone that we hear about, but don't know personally, whom we should strive to love for Allaah's sake.

_____

_____

_____

_____

_____

_____

_____

_____

_____

_____

_____

_____

_____

_____

_____

_____

_____

_____

_____

_____

DAY - 24

TEACHER NOTES / CORRECTIONS

_____

_____

_____

_____

_____

✴[/ 3]

08. Give a possible practical example of someone that we hear about, but don't know personally, whom we should have hatred towards for Allaah's sake.

_____

_____

_____

_____

_____

_____

_____

_____

_____

_____

_____

_____

_____

_____

_____

_____

_____

_____

_____

_____

_____

_____

_____

_____

DAY - 24

TEACHER NOTES / CORRECTIONS

_____

_____

_____

_____

_____

09. Discuss one possible negative effect of getting into the habit of generally speaking about religious matters from our opinions and perceptions.

_____

_____

_____

_____

_____

_____

_____

_____

_____

_____

_____

_____

_____

_____

_____

_____

_____

_____

_____

_____

_____

_____

DAY - 24

┌───┐
│   TEACHER NOTES / CORRECTIONS   │
└───┘

_____

_____

_____

_____

_____

✱[/ 3] = [/15]

TEST YOUR UNDERSTANDING:

TRUE & FALSE QUESTIONS

[Circle the correct letter for each individual sentence from today's content.]

3 min

01. The people we spend time with do not have any significant   [T / F]
    effect upon us.

02. There are no new religious innovations, only those which came   [T / F]
    about in the past.

03. The previous misguided sects found throughout Muslim   [T / F]
    history still exist today.

FILL IN THE BLANK QUESTIONS

[Enter the correct individual words to complete the sentences from today's content.]

6 min

04. Every form of _____ which existed previously is alive and

    _____ today in our age.

05. In addition to old forms of _____ , there are other _____
    forms of innovations and deviated beliefs today.

06. Success is being led by Allaah to _____ Him, and being blessed
    with _____ knowledge, and to do _____ deeds.

DAY - 25

COMPREHENSIVE UNDERSTANDING QUESTIONS

7-12 min

07. Give a practical example of one way that good companionship may influence a Muslim toward what is good and beneficial to him.

TEACHER NOTES / CORRECTIONS

DAY - 25

*[/ 3]

08. Give a practical example of one way in which bad companionship may influence a Muslim toward what is bad and harmful to him.

_____

_____

_____

_____

_____

_____

_____

_____

_____

_____

_____

_____

_____

_____

_____

_____

_____

_____

_____

_____

_____

_____

_____

_____

TEACHER NOTES / CORRECTIONS

_____

_____

_____

_____

_____

_____

09. Write down two misguided sects or groups which are found in the Muslim world today, and mention a Muslim country where that group or sect can be found.

_____

TEACHER NOTES / CORRECTIONS

*[/3]=[/15]

TEST YOUR UNDERSTANDING:

TRUE & FALSE QUESTIONS

[Circle the correct letter for each individual sentence from today's content.]

3 min

01. Allaah accepts all of our actions, as long as we are sincere in [T / F] doing them for Him.

02. From the dangers of innovation is the destruction of the rewards [T / F] of our good deeds.

03. There are conditions for the acceptance of our deeds by Allaah. [T / F]

FILL IN THE BLANK QUESTIONS

[Enter the correct individual words to complete the sentences from today's content.]

6 min

04. Both _____ sins and _____ in the religion may _____ a person towards major disbelief.

05. Allaah says that He will make the _____ of the _____ like scattered floating particles of dust.

06. The _____ innovator, whose innovation reaches the level of major _____ , is someone who none of their deeds will be _____ .

DAY - 26

COMPREHENSIVE UNDERSTANDING QUESTIONS

7-12 min

07.   Give a specific example of any sect or group whose innovation reaches the level of major disbelief, and so have been declared by the people of knowledge to be disbelievers.

_____

_____

_____

_____

_____

_____

_____

_____

_____

_____

_____

_____

_____

_____

_____

_____

_____

_____

_____

_____

_____

_____

TEACHER NOTES / CORRECTIONS

_____

_____

_____

_____

DAY - 26

*[/ 3]

08. Give a specific example of any sect or group whose innovation is below the level of major disbelief, and so are Muslims.

TEACHER NOTES / CORRECTIONS

09. Give a practical example of how someone might associate others with Allaah in their worship, and so have their deeds nullified and rejected.

TEACHER NOTES / CORRECTIONS

DAY - 26

✱[/3]=[/15]

TEST YOUR UNDERSTANDING:

TRUE & FALSE QUESTIONS

[Circle the correct letter for each individual sentence from today's content.]

3min

01. Even though innovations are misguidance, they are not disbelief.   [T / F]

02. A Muslim should free himself from any connection to every   [T / F]
form of misguidance.

03. Some of the astray sects have beliefs and practices that have   [T / F]
taken them outside of Islaam.

FILL IN THE BLANK QUESTIONS

[Enter the correct individual words to complete the sentences from today's content.]

6min

04. A knowledgeable Muslim should free himself from _____ statement
of _____ around him.

05. _____ yourself and turn away from every misguiding _____
which some people choose to follow.

06. Some matters of _____ innovation in the religion, cause an
individual to _____ Islaam.

DAY - 27

[/6]✷

COMPREHENSIVE UNDERSTANDING QUESTIONS

7-12 min

07. Give an example of one of the astray sects whose beliefs reach the level of major disbelief in Islaam. Describe that specific belief.

_____

_____

_____

_____

_____

_____

_____

_____

_____

_____

_____

_____

_____

_____

_____

_____

_____

_____

_____

_____

_____

_____

TEACHER NOTES / CORRECTIONS

_____

_____

DAY - 27

_____

_____

[/ 3]

08. Give an example of one of the misguided sects or groups who proceeds on innovation, which the scholars do not view as major disbelief. Describe that specific innovation they proceed upon.

TEACHER NOTES / CORRECTIONS

09. Give a specific example of any newly developed view or opinion some Muslims accept, which was unknown among the Companions of the Messenger of Allaah.

TEACHER NOTES / CORRECTIONS

DAY - 27

✳[/3]=[/15]

TEST YOUR UNDERSTANDING:

TRUE & FALSE QUESTIONS

[Circle the correct letter for each individual sentence from today's content.]

3min

01. It is acceptable to accommodate or support an innovator as   [T / F]
    long as you don't innovate yourself.

02. Innovating something new is blameworthy but not as bad as   [T / F]
    the many major sins people commit.

03. There is no clear way to tell what is considered a major sin by   [T / F]
    Allaah.

FILL IN THE BLANK QUESTIONS

[Enter the correct individual words to complete the sentences from today's content.]

6min

04. In this discussion what is intended by new _____ matters
    is: _____ .

05. The one who innovates a _____ matter in Islaam, has committed
    a major _____ .

06. The people of _____ and _____ are all those who bring
    new matters into the religion of Islaam.

DAY - 28

[/ 6]*

COMPREHENSIVE UNDERSTANDING QUESTIONS

7-12 min

07.   Give a specific example of something new related to giving da'wah that some people have innovated into Islaam.

_____

_____

_____

_____

_____

_____

_____

_____

_____

_____

_____

_____

_____

_____

_____

_____

_____

_____

_____

_____

_____

_____

_____

TEACHER NOTES / CORRECTIONS

_____

_____

DAY - 28

_____

_____

✳[/3]

08. Give a specific example of the mistake of protecting or accommodating an innovator in Islaam which a Muslim might fall into.

_____

_____

_____

_____

_____

_____

_____

_____

_____

_____

_____

_____

_____

_____

_____

_____

_____

_____

_____

_____

_____

_____

_____

_____

_____

TEACHER NOTES / CORRECTIONS

_____

_____

_____

_____

DAY - 28

_____

09. Explain a specific reason why some people might wrongly believe that making new matters in Islaam is something good.

TEACHER NOTES / CORRECTIONS

DAY - 28

*[/ 3]=[/15]

TEST YOUR UNDERSTANDING:

TRUE & FALSE QUESTIONS

[Circle the correct letter for each individual sentence from today's content.]

3min

01. The sin of innovation must be repented from like other sins   [T / F]
and transgressions.

02. Repentance from sin and transgression is only something in   [T / F]
the heart.

03. The Muslims judge other people according to their claims, not   [T / F]
their actions.

FILL IN THE BLANK QUESTIONS

[Enter the correct individual words to complete the sentences from today's content.]

6min

04. Ibn al-Mubaarak abandoned this man mentioned, due to his failure to

_____ make clear his _____ from previous misguidance
upon the way of the _____ .

05. The Jahmeeyah wrongly _____ the meanings and the reality of
Allaah's _____ and _____ .

06. It is a general obligation upon us to _____ the people of
innovation, and not to _____ with them or _____ with
them.

DAY - 29

COMPREHENSIVE UNDERSTANDING QUESTIONS

7-12 min

07.   Give a specific example of one way that a Muslim can make clear his repentance from innovation in our modern age.

_____

_____

_____

_____

_____

_____

_____

_____

_____

_____

_____

_____

_____

_____

_____

_____

_____

_____

_____

_____

_____

_____

_____

TEACHER NOTES / CORRECTIONS

_____

_____

_____

_____

DAY - 29

✳[/ 3]

08.   Name two possible things a Muslim must change, once he repents from some innovation which he previously accepted.

_____

_____

_____

_____

_____

_____

_____

_____

_____

_____

_____

_____

_____

_____

_____

_____

_____

_____

_____

_____

_____

_____

TEACHER NOTES / CORRECTIONS

_____

_____

_____

_____

DAY - 29

09. Give a possible example of how the scholars of the Sunnah might clarify the mistakes of the people of innovation in their society. Mention a specific example of when this has occurred.

TEACHER NOTES / CORRECTIONS

DAY - 29

*[/3]=[/15]

TEST YOUR UNDERSTANDING:

TRUE & FALSE QUESTIONS

[Circle the correct letter for each individual sentence from today's content.]

3 min

01. Maalik Ibn Anas, may Allaah have mercy upon him, was a well- [T / F] known leading scholar in the city of Mecca.

02. It is not possible to leave innovation that you fall into. [T / F]

03. The people of innovation have leaders who they take their [T / F] understanding and practice from.

FILL IN THE BLANK QUESTIONS

[Enter the correct individual words to complete the sentences from today's content.]

6 min

04. Abu 'Amaarah, was from the people of _____ in his time and a follower of his _____ .

05. Whatever we are cultivated upon when _____ , then most likely this is what we will _____ upon, except for those whom Allaah, in His mercy, guides.

06. The man who was _____ had this _____ towards Abu 'Amaarah, rather than being _____ to the Prophet Muhammad.

COMPREHENSIVE UNDERSTANDING QUESTIONS

7-12min

07.   Give an example of something that someone might say that indicates that their love of and connection to their leader is stronger than their love and connection to the Messenger of Allaah.

_____

_____

_____

_____

_____

_____

_____

_____

_____

_____

_____

_____

_____

_____

_____

_____

_____

_____

_____

_____

_____

_____

_____

TEACHER NOTES / CORRECTIONS

08. Give a possible reason or cause that might make it difficult for people of innovation to realize that they are not actually upon the religion of the Prophet as they claim.

TEACHER NOTES / CORRECTIONS

09. Give an example of a sect, group, or movement among the Muslims which people have a biased allegiance towards, which is greater than their attachment and allegiance to the Messenger of Allaah.

7-12 min

TEACHER NOTES / CORRECTIONS

DAY - 30

*[/3]=[/15]

THE NAKHLAH EDUCATIONAL SERIES:

The Purpose of the 'Nakhlah Educational Series' is to contribute to the present knowledge based efforts which enable Muslim individuals, families, and communities to understand and learn Islaam and then to develop within and truly live Islaam. Our commitment and goal is to contribute beneficial publications and works that:

Firstly, reflect the priority, message and methodology of all the prophets and messengers sent to humanity, meaning that single revealed message which embodies the very purpose of life, and of human creation. As Allaah the Most High has said,

❴ *We sent a Messenger to every nation ordering them that they should worship Allaah alone, obey Him and make their worship purely for Him, and that they should avoid everything worshipped besides Allaah. So from them there were those whom Allaah guided to His religion, and there were those who were unbelievers for whom misguidance was ordained. So travel through the land and see the destruction that befell those who denied the Messengers and disbelieved.* ❵–(Surah an-Nahl: 36)

Sheikh Rabee'a ibn Haadee al-Madkhalee in his work entitled, '*The Methodology of the Prophets in Calling to Allaah, That is the Way of Wisdom and Intelligence.*' explains the essential, enduring message of all the prophets:

"*So what was the message which these noble, chosen men, may Allaah's praises and salutations of peace be upon them all, brought to their people? Indeed their mission encompassed every matter of good and distanced and restrained every matter of evil. They brought forth to mankind everything needed for their well-being and happiness in this world and the Hereafter. There is nothing good except that they guided the people towards it, and nothing evil except that they warned the people against it. …*

This was the message found with all of the Messengers; that they should guide to every good and warn against every evil. However where did they start, what did they begin with and what did they concentrate upon? There are a number of essentials, basic principles, and fundamentals which all their calls were founded upon, and which were the starting point for calling the people to Allaah. These fundamental points and principles are: 1. The worship of Allaah alone without any associates 2. The sending of prophets to guide creation 3. The belief in the resurrection and the life of the Hereafter

These three principles are the area of commonality and unity within their calls, and stand as the fundamental principles which they were established upon. These principles are given the greatest importance in the Qur'aan and are fully explained in it. They are also its most important purpose upon which it centers and which it continually mentions. It further quotes intellectual and observable proofs for them in all its chapters as well as within most of its accounts of previous nations and given examples.

This is known to those who have full understanding, and are able to consider carefully and comprehend well. All the Books revealed by Allaah have given great importance to these points and all of the various revealed laws of guidance are agreed upon them. And the most important and sublime of these three principles, and the most fundamental of them all is directing one's worship only towards Allaah alone, the Blessed and the Most High."

Today one finds that there are indeed many paths, groups, and organizations apparently presenting themselves as representing Islaam, which struggle to put forth an outwardly pleasing appearance to the general Muslims; but when their methods are placed upon the precise scale of conforming to priorities and methodology of the message of the prophets sent by Allaah, they can only be recognized as deficient paths- not simply in practice but in principle- leading not to success but rather only to inevitable failure. As Sheikh Saaleh al-Fauzaan, may Allaah preserve him, states in his introduction to the same above mentioned work on the methodology of all the prophets,

"So whichever call is not built upon these foundations, and whatever methodology is not from the methodology of the Messengers - then it will be frustrated and fail, and it will be effort and toil without any benefit. The clearest proofs of this are those present day groups and organizations which set out a methodology and program for themselves and their efforts of calling the people to Islaam which is different from the methodology of the Messengers. These groups have neglected the importance of the people having the correct belief and creed - except for a very few of them - and instead call for the correction of side-issues."

There can be no true success in any form for us as individuals, families, or larger communities without making the encompassing worship of Allaah alone, with no partners or associates, the very and only foundation of our lives. It is necessary that each individual knowingly choose to base his life upon that same foundation taught by all the prophets and messengers sent by the Lord of all the worlds, rather than simply delving into the assorted secondary concerns and issues invited to by the various numerous parties, innovated movements, and groups. Indeed Sheikh al-Albaanee, may Allaah have mercy upon him, stated:

*"... We unreservedly combat against this way of having various different parties and groups. As this false way- of group or organizational allegiances - conforms to the statement of Allaah the Most High, ﴾ **But they have broken their religion among them into sects, each group rejoicing in what is with it as its beliefs. And every party is pleased with whatever they stand with.**﴿–(Surah al-Mu'minoon: 53) And in truth they are no separate groups and parties in Islaam itself. There is only one true party, as is stated in a verse in the Qur'an, ﴾ **Verily, it is the party of Allaah that will be the successful.** ﴿–(Surah al-Mujadilaah: 58). The party of Allaah are those people who stand with the Messenger of Allaah, may Allaah's praise and salutations be upon him, meaning that an individual proceeds upon the methodology of the Companions of the Messenger. Due to this we call for having sound knowledge of the Book and the Sunnah."*

(Knowledge Based Issues & Sharee'ah Rulings: The Rulings of The Guiding Scholar Sheikh Muhammad Naasiruddeen al-Albaanee Made in the City of Medina & In the Emirates – [Emiratee Fatwa no 114. P.30])

Secondly, building upon the above foundation, our commitment is to contributing publications and works which reflect the inherited message and methodology of the acknowledged scholars of the many various branches of Sharee'ah knowledge who stood upon the straight path of preserved guidance in every century and time since the time of our Messenger, may Allaah's praise and salutations be upon him. These people of knowledge, who are the inheritors of the Final Messenger, have always adhered closely to the two revealed sources of guidance: the Book of Allaah and the Sunnah of the Messenger of Allaah- may Allaah's praise and salutations be upon him, upon the united consensus, standing with the body of guided Muslims in every century - preserving and transmitting the true religion generation after generation. Indeed the Messenger of Allaah, may Allaah's praise and salutations be upon him, informed us that, *{ A group of people amongst my Ummah will remain obedient to Allaah's orders. They will not be harmed by those who leave them nor by those who oppose them, until Allaah's command for the Last Day comes upon them while they remain on the right path. }* (Authentically narrated in Saheeh al-Bukhaaree).

We live in an age in which the question frequently asked is, "*How do we make Islaam a reality?*" and perhaps the related and more fundamental question is, "*What is Islaam?*", such that innumerable different voices quickly stand to offer countless different conflicting answers through books, lectures, and every available form of modern media. Yet the only true course of properly understanding this question and its answer- for ourselves and our families -is to return to the criterion given to us by our beloved Messenger, may Allaah's praise and salutations be upon him. Indeed the Messenger of Allaah, may Allaah's praise and salutations be upon him, indicated in an authentic narration, clarifying the matter beyond doubt, that the only "Islaam" which enables one to be truly successful and saved in this world and the next is as he said, *{... that which I am upon and my Companions are upon today.}* (authentically narrated in Jaam'ea at-Tirmidhee) referring to that Islaam which stands upon unchanging revealed knowledge. While every other changed and altered form of Islaam, whether through some form of extremism or negligence, or through the addition or removal of something, regardless of whether that came from a good intention or an evil one- is not the religion that Allaah informed us abou when He revealed, ❖ *This day, those who disbelieved have given up all hope of your religion; so fear them not, but fear Me. This day, I have perfected your religion for you, completed My Favor upon you, and have chosen for you Islaam as your religion.*❖–(Surah al-Maa'idah: 3)

The guiding scholar Sheikh al-Albaanee, may have mercy upon him, said,

"*...And specifically mentioning those among the callers who have taken upon themselves the guiding of the young Muslim generation upon Islaam, working to educate them with its education, and to socialize them with its culture. Yet they themselves have generally not attempted to unify their understanding of those matters about Islaam regarding which the people of Islaam today differ about so severely.*

MISSION

And the situation is certainly not as is falsely supposed by some individuals from among them who are heedless or negligent - that the differences that exist among them are only in secondary matters without entering into or affecting the fundamental issues or principles of the religion; and the examples to prove that this is not true are numerous and recognized by those who have studied the books of the many differing groups and sects, or by the one who has knowledge of the various differing concepts and beliefs held by the Muslims today."(Mukhtasir al-'Uloo Lil'Alee al-Ghafaar, page 55)

Similarly he, may Allaah have mercy upon him, explained:

"Indeed, Islaam is the only solution, and this statement is something which the various different Islamic groups, organizations, and movements could never disagree about. And this is something which is from the blessings of Allaah upon the Muslims. However there are significant differences between the different Islamic groups, organizations, and movements that are present today regarding that domain which working within will bring about our rectification. What is that area of work to endeavor within, striving to restore a way of life truly reflecting Islaam, renewing that system of living which comes from Islaam, and in order to establish the Islamic government? The groups and movements significantly differ upon this issue or point. Yet we hold that it is required to begin with the matters of tasfeeyah —clarification, and tarbeeyah -education and cultivation, with both of them being undertaken together.

As if we were to start with the issue of governing and politics, then it has been seen that those who occupy themselves with this focus firstly posses beliefs which are clearly corrupted and ruined, and secondly that their personal behavior, from the aspect of conforming to Islaam, is very far from conforming to the actual guidance of the Sharee'ah. While those who first concern themselves with working just to unite the people and gather the masses together under a broad banner of the general term "Islaam", then it is seen that within the minds of those speakers who raise such calls -in reality there is fact no actual clear understanding of what Islaam is. Moreover, the understanding they have of Islaam has no significant impact in starting to change and reform their own lives. Due to this reason you find that many such individuals from here and there, who hold this perspective, are unable to truly realize or reflect Islaam even in areas of their own personal lives in matters which it is in fact easily possible for them to implement. As he holds that no one - regardless of whether it is because of his arrogance or pridefulness - can enter into directing him in an area of his personal life!

Yet at the same time these same individuals are raising their voices saying, "Judgment is only for Allaah!" and "It is required that judgment of affairs be according to what Allaah revealed." And this is indeed a true statement. But the one who does not possess something certainly cannot give or offer it to others. The majority of Muslims today have not established the judgment of Allaah fully upon themselves, yet they still seek from others to establish the judgment of Allaah within their governments...

...And I understand that this issue or subject is not immune from there being those who oppose our methodology of tasfeeyah and tarbeeyah. As there is the one who would say, "But establishing this tasfeeyah and tarbeeyah is a matter which requires many long years!" So, I respond by saying, this is not an important consideration in this matter, what is important is that we carry out what we have been commanded to do within our religion and by our Mighty Lord. What is important is that we begin by properly understanding our religion first and foremost. After this is accomplished then it will not be important whether the road itself is long or short.

*And indeed I direct this statement of mine towards those men who are callers to the religion among the Muslims, and towards the scholars and those who direct our affairs. I call for them to stand upon complete knowledge of true Islaam, and to fight against every form of negligence and heedlessness regarding the religion, and against differing and disputes, as Allaah has said, ❴...**and do not dispute with one another for fear that you lose courage and your strength departs**❵—(Surah Al-Anfaal: 46).*

(Quoted from the work, 'The Life of Sheikh al-Albaanee, His Influence in Present Day Fields of Sharee'ah Knowledge, & the Praise of the Scholars for Him.' volume 1 page 380-385)

The guiding scholar Sheikh Zayd al-Madkhalee, may Allaah protect him, stated in his writing, 'The Well Established Principles of the Way of the First Generations of Muslims: It's Enduring & Excellent Distinct Characteristics' that,

"From among these principles and characteristics is that the methodology of tasfeeyah -or clarification, and tarbeeyah -or education and cultivation- is clearly affirmed and established as a true way coming from the first three generations of Islaam, and is something well known to the people of true merit from among them, as is concluded by considering all the related evidence. What is intended by tasfeeyah, when referring to it generally, is clarifying that which is the truth from that which is falsehood, what is goodness from that which is harmful and corrupt, and when referring to its specific meanings it is distinguishing the noble Sunnah of the Prophet and the people of the Sunnah from those innovated matters brought into the religion and the people who are supporters of such innovations.

As for what is intended by tarbeeyah, it is calling all of the creation to take on the manners and embrace the excellent character invited to by that guidance revealed to them by their Lord through His worshiper and Messenger Muhammad, may Allaah's praise and salutations be upon him; so that they might have good character, manners, and behavior. As without this they cannot have a good life, nor can they put right their present condition or their final destination. And we seek refuge in Allaah from the evil of not being able to achieve that rectification."

Thus the methodology of the people of standing upon the Prophet's Sunnah, and proceeding upon the 'way of the believers' in every century is reflected in a focus and concern with these two essential matters: tasfeeyah or clarification of what is original, revealed message from the Lord of all the worlds, and tarbeeyah or education and raising of ourselves, our families, and our communities, and our lands upon what has been distinguished to be that true message and path.

MISSION

The Roles of the Scholars & General Muslims In Raising the New Generation

The priority and focus of the 'Nakhlah Educational Series' is reflected within in the following statements of Sheikh al-Albaanee, may Allaah have mercy upon him:

"As for the other obligation, then I intend by this the education of the young generation upon Islaam purified from all of those impurities we have mentioned, giving them a correct Islamic education from their very earliest years, without any influence of a foreign, disbelieving education."
(Silsilat al-Hadeeth ad-Da'eefah, Introduction page 2.)

"...And since the Messenger of Allaah, may Allaah's praise and salutations be upon him, has indicated that the only cure to remove this state of humiliation that we find ourselves entrenched within, is truly returning back to the religion. Then it is clearly obligatory upon us - through the people of knowledge- to correctly and properly understand the religion in a way that conforms to the sources of the Book of Allaah and the Sunnah, and that we educate and raise a new virtuous, righteous generation upon this."
(Clarification and Cultivation and the Need of the Muslims for Them)

It is essential in discussing our perspective upon this obligation of raising the new generation of Muslims, that we highlight and bring attention to a required pillar of these efforts as indicated by Sheikh al-Albaanee, may Allaah have mercy upon him, and others- in the golden words, *"through the people of knowledge"*. Since something we commonly experience today is that many people have various incorrect understandings of the role that the scholars should have in the life of a Muslim, failing to understand the way in which they fulfill their position as the inheritors of the Messenger of Allaah, may Allaah's praise and salutations be upon him, and stand as those who preserve and enable us to practice the guidance of Islaam. Indeed, the noble Imaam Sheikh as-Sa'dee, may Allaah have mercy upon him, in his work, *"A Definitive and Clear Explanation of the Work 'A Triumph for the Saved Sect'"* pages 237-240, has explained this crucial issue with an extraordinary explanation full of remarkable benefits:

"Section: Explaining the Conditions for These Two Source Texts to Suffice You -or the Finding of Sufficiency in these Two Sources of Revelation.
Overall the conditions needed to achieve this and bring it about return to two matters:
Firstly, the presence of the requirements necessary for achieving this; meaning a complete devotion to the Book and the Sunnah, and the putting forth of efforts both in seeking to understand their intended meanings, as well as in striving to be guided by them. What is required secondly is the pushing away of everything which prevents achieving this finding of sufficiency in them.

This is through having a firm determination to distance yourself from everything which contradicts these two source texts in what comes from the historical schools of jurisprudence, assorted various statements, differing principles and their resulting conclusions which the majority of people proceed upon. These matters which contradict the two sources of revelation include many affairs which, when the worshiper of Allaah repels them from himself and stands against them, the realm of his knowledge, understanding, and deeds then expands greatly. Through a devotion to them and a complete dedication towards these two sources of revelation, proceeding upon every path which assists one's understanding them, and receiving enlightenment from the light of the scholars and being guided by the guidance that they possess- you will achieve that complete sufficiency in them. And surely, in the positions they take towards the leading people of knowledge and the scholars, the people are three types of individuals:

The first of them is the one who goes to extremes in his attachment to the scholars. He makes their statements something which are infallible as if their words held the same position as those of the statements of the Messenger of Allaah, may Allaah's praise and salutations be upon him, as well as giving those scholars' statements precedence and predominance over the Book of Allaah and the Sunnah. This is despite the fact that every leading scholar who has been accepted by this Ummah was one who promoted and encouraged the following of the Book and the Sunnah, commanding the people not to follow their own statements nor their school of thought in anything which stood in opposition to the Book of Allaah and the Sunnah.

The second type is the one who generally rejects and invalidates the statements of the scholars and forbids the referring to the statements of the leading scholars of guidance and those people of knowledge who stand as brilliant lamps in the darkness. This type of person neither relies upon the light of discernment with the scholars, nor utilizes their stores of knowledge. Or even if perhaps they do so, they do not direct thanks towards them for this. And this manner and way prohibits them from tremendous good. Furthermore, that which motivates such individuals to proceed in this way is their falsely supposing that the obligation to follow the Messenger of Allaah, may Allaah's praise and salutations be upon him, and the giving of precedence to his statements over the statements of anyone else, requires that they do without any reliance upon the statements of the Companions, or those who followed them in goodness, or those leading scholars of guidance within the Ummah. And this is a glaring and extraordinary mistake.

As indeed the Companions and the people of knowledge are the means and the agency between the Messenger of Allaah, may Allaah's praise and salutations be upon him, and his Ummah- in the transmission and spreading his Sunnah in regard to both its wording and texts as well as its meanings and understanding. Therefore the one who follows them in what they convey in this is guided through their understandings, receives knowledge from the light they possess, benefits from the conclusions they have derived from these sources -of beneficial meanings and explanations, as well as in relation to subtle matters which scarcely occur to the minds of some of the other people of knowledge, or barely comes to be discerned by their minds. Consequently, from the blessing of Allaah upon this Ummah is that He has given them these guiding scholars who cultivate and educate them upon two clear types of excellent cultivation.

MISSION

The first category is education from the direction of ones knowledge and understanding. They educate the Ummah upon the more essential and fundamental matters before the more complex affairs. They convey the meanings of the Book and the Sunnah to the minds and intellects of the people through efforts of teaching which rectifies, and through composing various beneficial books of knowledge which a worshiper doesn't even have the ability to adequately describe what is encompassed within them of aspects of knowledge and benefits. Works which reflect the presence of a clear white hand in deriving guidance from the Book of Allaah and the Sunnah, and through the arrangement, detailed clarification, division and explanation, through the gathering together of explanations, comparisons, conditions, pillars, and explanations about that which prevents the fulfillment of matters, as well as distinguishing between differing meanings and categorizing various knowledge based benefits.

The second category is education from the direction of ones conduct and actions. They cultivate the peoples characters encouraging them towards every praiseworthy aspect of good character, through explaining its ruling and high status, and what benefits comes to be realized from it, clarifying the reasons and paths which enable one to attain it, as well as those affairs which prevent, delay or hinder someone becoming one distinguished and characterized by it. Because they, in reality, are those who bring nourishment to the hearts and the souls; they are the doctors who treat the diseases of the heart and its defects. As such they educate the people through their statements, actions as well as their general guided way. Therefore the scholars have a tremendous right over this Ummah. The portion of love and esteem, respect and honor, and thanks due to them because their merits and their various good efforts stand above every other right after establishing the right of Allaah, and the right of His Messenger, may Allaah's praise and salutations be upon him.

Because of this, the third group of individuals in respect to the scholars are those who have been guided to understand their true role and position, and establish their rights, thanking them for their virtues and merits, benefiting by taking from the knowledge they have, while acknowledging their rank and status. They understand that the scholars are not infallible and that their statements must stand in conformance to the statements of the Messenger of Allaah, may Allaah's praise and salutations be upon him. And that each one from among them has that which is from guidance, knowledge, and correctness in his statements taken and benefited from, while turning away from whatever in mistaken within it.

Yet such a scholar is not to be belittled for his mistake, as he stands as one who strove to reach the truth; therefore his mistake will be forgiven, and he should be thanked for his efforts. One clarifies what was stated by of any one of these leaders from among men, when it is recognizes that it has some weakness or conflict to an evidence of the Sharee'ah, by explaining its weakness and the level of that weakness, without speaking evilly of the intention of those people of knowledge and religion, nor defaming them due to that error. Rather we say, as it is obligatory to say, "And those who came after them say: ❴ **Our Lord! forgive us and our brethren who have preceded us in faith, and put not in our hearts any hatred against those who have believed. Our Lord! You are indeed full of kindness, Most Merciful.** ❵ -(Surah al-Hashr: 10).

Accordingly, individuals of this third type are those who fulfill two different matters. They join together on one hand between giving precedence to the Book and the Sunnah over everything else, and, on the other hand, between comprehending the level and position of the scholars and the leading people of knowledge and guidance, and establishing this even if it is only done in regard to some of their rights upon us. So we ask Allaah to bless us to be from this type, and to make us from among the people of this third type, and to make us from those who love Him and love those who love Him, and those who love every action which brings us closer to everything He loves."

Upon this clarity regarding the proper understanding of our balanced position towards our guided Muslim scholars, consider the following words about the realm of work of the general people of faith, which explains our area of efforts and struggle as Muslim parents, found in the following statement by Sheikh Saaleh Fauzaan al-Fauzaan, may Allaah preserve him.

"Question: Some people mistakenly believe that calling to Allaah is a matter not to be undertaken by anyone else other than the scholars without exception, and that it is not something required for other than the scholars according to that which they have knowledge of -to undertake any efforts of calling the people to Allaah. So what is your esteemed guidance regarding this?" The Sheikh responded by saying:

"This is not a misconception, but is in fact a reality. The call to Allaah cannot be established except through those who are scholars. And I state this. Yet, certainly there are clear issues which every person understands. As such, every individual should enjoin the good and forbid wrongdoing according to the level of his understanding. Such that he instructs and orders the members of his household to perform the ritual daily prayers and other matters that are clear and well known.

*Undertaking this is something mandatory and required even upon the common people, such that they must command their children to perform their prayers in the masjid. The Messenger of Allaah, may Allaah praise and salutations be upon him, said, { **Command you children to pray at seven, and beat them due to its negligence at ten.**} (Authentic narration found in Sunan Abu Dawood). And the Messenger of Allaah, may Allaah praise and salutations be upon him, said, { **Each one of you is a guardian or a shepherd, and each of you is responsible for those under his guardianship....**} (Authentic narration found in Saheeh al-Bukhaaree). So this is called guardianship, and this is also called enjoining the good and forbidding wrongdoing. The Messenger of Allaah, may Allaah praise and salutations be upon him, said, { **The one from among you who sees a wrong should change it with his hand, and if he is unable to do so, then with his tongue, and if he is not able to do this, then with his heart. }** (Authentic narration found in Saheeh Muslim).*

So in relation to the common person, that which it is required from him to endeavor upon is that he commands the members of his household-as well as others -with the proper performance of the ritual prayers, the obligatory charity, with generally striving to obey Allaah, and to stay away from sins and transgressions, and that he purify and cleanse his home from disobedience, and that he educate and cultivate his children upon the obedience of Allaah's commands. This is what is required from him, even if he is a general person. As these types of matters are from that which is understood by every single person. This is something which is clear and apparent.

MISSION

But as for the matters of putting forth rulings and judgments regarding matters in the religion, or entering into clarifying issues of what is permissible and what is forbidden, or explaining what is considered associating others in the worship due to Allaah and what is properly worshiping Him alone without any partner- then indeed these are matters which cannot be established except by the scholars"

(Beneficial Responses to Questions About Modern Methodologies, Question 15, page 22)

Similarly the guiding scholar Sheikh 'Abdul-'Azeez Ibn Baaz, may Allaah have mercy upon him, also emphasized this same overall responsibility:

*"...It is also upon a Muslim that he struggles diligently in that which will place his worldly affairs in a good state, just as he must also strive in the correcting of his religious affairs and the affairs of his own family. As the people of his household have a significant right over him that he strive diligently in rectifying their affair and guiding them towards goodness, due to the statement of Allaah, the Most Exalted, ❦ **Oh you who believe! Save yourselves and your families Hellfire whose fuel is men and stones** ❧ -(Surah at-Tahreem: 6)*

*So it is upon you to strive to correct the affairs of the members of your family. This includes your wife, your children- both male and female- and such as your own brothers. This concerns all of the people in your family, meaning you should strive to teach them the religion, guiding and directing them, and warning them from those matters Allaah has prohibited for us. Because you are the one who is responsible for them as shown in the statement of the Prophet, may Allaah's praise and salutations be upon him, { **Every one of you is a guardian, and responsible for what is in his custody. The ruler is a guardian of his subjects and responsible for them; a husband is a guardian of his family and is responsible for it; a lady is a guardian of her husband's house and is responsible for it, and a servant is a guardian of his master's property and is responsible for it....}** Then the Messenger of Allaah, may Allaah's praise and salutations be upon him, continued to say, { **...so all of you are guardians and are responsible for those under your authority.}** (Authentically narrated in Saheeh al-Bukhaaree & Muslim)*

It is upon us to strive diligently in correcting the affairs of the members of our families, from the aspect of purifying their sincerity of intention for Allaah's sake alone in all of their deeds, and ensuring that they truthfully believe in and follow the Messenger of Allaah, may Allaah's praise and salutations be upon him, their fulfilling the prayer and the other obligations which Allaah the Most Exalted has commanded for us, as well as from the direction of distancing them from everything which Allaah has prohibited.

*It is upon every single man and women to give advice to their families about the fulfillment of what is obligatory upon them. Certainly, it is upon the woman as well as upon the man to perform this. In this way our homes become corrected and rectified in regard to the most important and essential matters. Allaah said to His Prophet, may Allaah's praise and salutations be upon him, ❦ **And enjoin the ritual prayers on your family...** ❧ (Surah Taha: 132) Similarly, Allaah the Most Exalted said to His prophet Ismaa'aeel, ❦ **And mention in the Book, Ismaa'aeel. Verily, he was true to what he promised, and he was a Messenger, and a Prophet. And he used to enjoin on his family and his people the ritual prayers and the obligatory charity, and his Lord was pleased with him.** ❧ -(Surah Maryam: 54-55)*

As such, it is only proper that we model ourselves after the prophets and the best of people, and be concerned with the state of the members of our households. Do not be neglectful of them, oh worshipper of Allaah! Regardless of whether it is concerning your wife, your mother, father, grandfather, grandmother, your brothers, or your children; it is upon you to strive diligently in correcting their state and condition..."

(Collection of Various Rulings and Statements- Sheikh 'Abdul-'Azeez Ibn 'Abdullah Ibn Baaz, Vol. 6, page 47)

CONTENT & STRUCTURE:

We hope to contribute works which enable every striving Muslim who acknowledges the proper position of the scholars, to fulfill the recognized duty and obligation which lays upon each one of us to bring the light of Islaam into our own lives as individuals as well as into our homes and among our families. Towards this goal we are committed to developing educational publications and comprehensive educational curricula -through cooperation with and based upon the works of the scholars of Islaam and the students of knowledge. Works which, with the assistance of Allaah, the Most High, we can utilize to educate and instruct ourselves, our families and our communities upon Islaam in both principle and practice. The publications and works of the Nakhlah Educational Series are divided into the following categories:

Basic / Elementary: Ages 4-11
Secondary: Ages 11-14
High School: Ages 14- Young Adult
General: Young Adult –Adult
Supplementary: All Ages

Publications and works within these stated levels will, with the permission of Allaah, encompass different beneficial areas and subjects, and will be offered in every permissible form of media and medium. As certainly, as the guiding scholar Sheikh Saaleh Fauzaan al-Fauzaan, may Allaah preserve him, has stated,

"Beneficial knowledge is itself divided into two categories. Firstly is that knowledge which is tremendous in its benefit, as it benefits in this world and continues to benefit in the Hereafter. This is religious Sharee'ah knowledge. And secondly, that which is limited and restricted to matters related to the life of this world, such as learning the processes of manufacturing various goods. This is a category of knowledge related specifically to worldly affairs.

...As for the learning of worldly knowledge, such as knowledge of manufacturing, then it is legislated upon us collectively to learn whatever the Muslims have a need for. Yet, if they do not have a need for this knowledge, then learning it is a neutral matter upon the condition that it does not compete with or displace any areas of Sharee'ah knowledge..."

("Explanations of the Mistakes of Some Writers", Pages 10-12)

So we strive always to remind ourselves and our brothers of this crucial point also indicated by Sheikh Sadeeq Ibn Hasan al-Qanoojee, may Allaah have mercy upon him, in: *'Abjad al-'Uloom'*, (page 89)

MISSION

"...What is intended by knowledge in the mentioned hadeeth is knowledge of the religion and the distinctive Sharee'ah, knowledge of the Noble Book and the pure Sunnah, of which there is no third along with them. But what is not meant in this narration are those invented areas of knowledge, whether they emerged in previous ages or today's world, which the people in these present times have devoted themselves to. They have specifically dedicated themselves to them in a manner which prevents them from looking towards those areas of knowledge related to faith, and in a way which has preoccupied them from occupying themselves from what is actually wanted or desired by Allaah, the Most High, and His Messenger, who is the leader of men and Jinn. Such that the knowledge in the Qur'aan has become something abandoned and the sciences of hadeeth have become obscure. While these new areas of knowledge related to manufacturing and production continually emerge from the nations of disbelief and apostasy, and they are called, "sciences", "arts", and "ideal development". And this sad state increases every day, indeed from Allaah we came and to Him shall we return....

...Additionally, although the various areas of beneficial knowledge all share some level of value, they all have differing importance and ranks. Among them is that which is to be considered according to its subject, such as medicine, and its subject is the human body. Or such as the sciences of 'tafseer' and its subject is the explanation of the words of Allaah, the Most Exalted and Most High, and the value of these two areas is not in any way unrecognized.

And from among the various areas there are those areas which are considered according to their objective, such as knowledge of upright character, and its goal is understanding the beneficial merits that an individual can come to possess. And from among them there are those areas which are considered according to the people's need for them, such as 'fiqh' which the need for it is urgent and essential. And from among them there are those areas which are considered according to their apparent strength, such as knowledge of physical sports and exercise, as it is something openly demonstrated.

And from the areas of knowledge are those areas which rise in their position of importance through their combining all these different matters within them, or the majority of them. Such as revealed religious knowledge, as its subject is indeed esteemed, its objective one of true merit, and its need is undeniably felt. Likewise one area of knowledge may be considered of superior rank than another in consideration of the results that it brings forth, or the strength of its outward manifestation, or due to the essentialness of its objective. Similarly the result that an area produces is certainly of higher estimation and significance in appraisal than the outward or apparent significance of some other areas of knowledge.

For that reason the highest ranking and most valuable area of knowledge is that of knowledge of Allaah the Most Perfect and the Most High, of His angels, and messengers, and all the particulars of these beliefs, as its result is that of eternal and continuing happiness."

We ask Allaah, the most High to bless us with success in contributing to the many efforts of our Muslim brothers and sisters committed to raising themselves as individuals and the next generation of our children upon that Islaam which Allaah has perfected and chosen for us, and which He has enabled the guided Muslims to proceed upon in each and every century. We ask him to forgive us, and forgive the Muslim men and the Muslim women, and to guide all the believers to everything He loves and is pleased with. The success is from Allaah, The Most High The Most Exalted, alone and all praise is due to Him.

Abu Sukhailah Khalil Ibn-Abelahyi
Taalib al-Ilm Educational Resources

Taalib al-Ilm Educational Publications is looking for

Distributors:

We are working to make Taalib al-Ilm Education Resources publications available through distributors worldwide. Our present discounts for wholesalers are:

50% discount for any order of **USD $2000** or over retail cost

60% discount for any order of **USD $5000** or over retail cost

For further information, please contact the sales department by e-mail: *service@taalib.com.*

Publication Contributors:

Additionally, in an effort to further expand our publication library, we are seeking contributing authors, translators, and compilers with beneficial works of any area of Sharee'ah knowledge for submission of their works for potential publication by us. For details and all submission guidelines please email us at: *service@taalib.com*

Referral bonus: *Individuals who refer a new distributor or publication contributor to us can receive a **$25 PayPal payment** upon:*

1) a confirmed contract with a publication contributor or

2) receipt of a newly referred distributor's initial order at the 50% discount level.

Contact us for further information and conditions.

MISSION

30 Days of Guidance:
Cultivating The Character & Behavior of Islaam

A Short Journey Within The Work Al-Adab Al-Mufrad With

Sheikh Zayd Ibn Muhammad Ibn Haadee al-Madhkhaalee
(may Allaah have mercy on him)

*Do you understand the nature of Islaam? * What do you have that is equal to this world? * Are you wealthy? * Are you prepared for your reckoning? * Are you always working for good while you can? * Do you remember the benefit in your difficulties? * Which of these two pairs has a greater influence in your life? * Whom do you really love and why? * Who are your close friends? * Do you protect yourself from the harm of others? * Are you a miser or someone who is incapable? * Do you know the best of supplications? * Do you ask Allaah's protection from your own evil? * Do you seek refuge from bad conditions and worship at night? * Do you know which trials contain some betterment for you? * Do you supplicate for your family as both a parent and as a child? * How well do you treat your mother and father? * How do you fulfill your responsibilities towards your household? * Do you know who are the best and worst of Muslim women? * Is your life balanced as was the lives of the Companions? * Do you understand how to give the best of charity? * How do you spend your money? * How many ways of giving charity and doing good do you do * How are you towards your neighbors? * How do you deal with your own faults and those of others? * How do you treat younger Muslims? * How do you interact with other Muslims? * Do you work to change your bad habits? * Do you know the benefits of maintaining family ties? * Do you know what things bring you closer to Jannah?*

Compiled and Translated by:

Abu Sukhailah Khalil Ibn-Abelahyi

[Available: **Now** ¦ price: **(SS) $27.50 (DS) $25 (W) $12** ¦ **(Kindle) $9.99**]

An Educational Course Based Upon:

Beneficial Answers to Questions On Innovated Methodologies

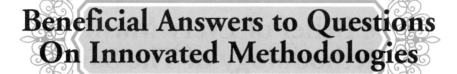

By the Guiding Scholar

Sheikh Saaleh Ibn Abdullah al-Fauzaan
(may Allaah preserve him)

This course focuses upon the importance of clarity in the way you understand and practice Islaam, in the midst of today's confusing claims to Islaam.

What is the right way or methodology, to practice Islaam? Examine evidences and proofs from the sources texts of the Qur'aan and Sunnah along with the statements of many scholars explaining them, which connect you directly to that Islaam which the Messenger of Allaah ﷺ taught his Companions, may Allaah be pleased with them all.

Course Features:

Twenty concise illustrated lessons to facilitate learning & review with several important textual & course appendices.

Compiled and Translated by:

Abu Sukhailah Khalil Ibn-Abelahyi

[Available: **Now** ¦ price: **(SS) $35 (DS) $32.50 (W) $12** ¦ **(Kindle) $9.99**]

Lessons & Benefits From the Two Excellent Works:

The Belief of Every Muslim & The Methodology of The Saved Sect

By the Guiding Scholar
Sheikh Muhammad Ibn Jameel Zaynoo
(may Allaah preserve him)

This course begins with three full lessons with specific practical guidelines on how to effectively study Islaam and gain the knowledge needed to build your life as a Muslim into a life which is pleasing to Allaah.

Through twenty lessons on knowledge, beliefs, & methodology along with quizzes, review questions & lesson benefits -the remaining lessons take simply explained passages from two beneficial works that cover many important principles and the common misconceptions connected to them, which are fundamental to correctly understanding Islaam as it was taught to the Companions of the Messenger of Allaah.

Compiled and Translated by:

Abu Sukhailah Khalil Ibn-Abelahyi

[Available: **Now** ¦ price: (SS) $27.50 (DS) $25
(W) $12 ¦ (Kindle) $9.99]

Statements of the Guiding Scholars of Our Age

Regarding Books & their Advice to the Beginner Seeker of Knowledge

with Selections from the Following Scholars:

Sheikh 'Abdul-'Azeez ibn 'Abdullah ibn Baaz -Sheikh Muhammad ibn Saaleh al-'Utheimein - Sheikh Muhammad Naasiruddeen al-Albaanee - Sheikh Muqbil ibn Haadee al-Waada'ee - Sheikh 'Abdur-Rahman ibn Naaser as-Sa'adee - Sheikh Muhammad 'Amaan al-Jaamee - Sheikh Muhammad al-Ameen as-Shanqeetee - Sheikh Ahmad ibn Yahya an-Najmee
(May Allaah have mercy upon them)

Sheikh Saaleh al-Fauzaan ibn 'Abdullah al-Fauzaan - Sheikh Saaleh ibn 'Abdul-'Azeez Aal-Sheikh - Sheikh Muhammad ibn 'Abdul-Wahhab al-Wasaabee -Permanent Committee to Scholastic Research & Issuing Of Islamic Rulings
(May Allaah preserve them.)

Book Sections:

1. Guidance and Direction for Every Male and Female Muslim

2. Golden Advice that Benefits the Beginner Regarding Acquiring Knowledge

3. Beneficial Guidance for Female Students of Sharee'ah Knowledge

4 Guidance from the Scholars Regarding Important Books to Acquire for Seeking Knowledge

5. The Warning of the Scholars from the Books of those who have Deviated & the Means and Ways of Going Astray

6. Clear Statements from the Scholars' Advice Regarding Memorizing Knowledge

7. Issues Related to the Verifiers of Books in our Age

Compiled and Translated by:
Abu Sukhailah Khalil Ibn-Abelahyi

[Available: **Now** ¦ price: **(HB) $32.50 (SB) $25** ¦ **(Kindle) $9.99**]

The Cure, The Explanation, The Clear Affair, & The Brilliantly Distinct Signpost [1]

A Step by Step Educational Course on Islaam
Based upon Commentaries of

'Usul as-Sunnah' of Imaam Ahmad
(may Allaah have mercy upon him)

This initial course book, which is part of a full series, can be vital learning tool, by Allah's persmission, for discussing and learning many of the most important beliefs of Islaam, how to implement them, and how to avoid common mistakes and misunderstandings. This full course series is based upon various commentaries of the original text, from the following scholars of our age, may Allaah preserve them all:

- Sheikh Zayd Ibn Muhammad al-Madkhalee
- Sheikh Saleeh Ibn Sa'd As-Suhaaymee
- Sheikh 'Abdul-'Azeez Ibn 'Abdullah ar-Raajhee
- Sheikh Rabee'a Ibn Haadee al-Madkhalee
- Sheikh Sa'd Ibn Naasir as-Shathree
- Sheikh 'Ubayd Ibn 'Abdullah al-Jaabiree
- Sheikh 'Abdullah Al-Bukharee
- Sheikh Hamaad Uthmaan

Each course book lesson has: lesson text, scholastic commentary, evidence summary, lesson benefits, standard & review exercises, as well as the Arabic text & translation of 'Usul as-Sunnah' in Arabic divided for easier memorization.

Compiled and Translated by:

Abu Sukhailah Khalil Ibn-Abelahyi

[Available: **TBA**¦ price: **(SS) $30 (DS) $27.50 (W) $12** ¦ **(Kindle) $9.99**]

Whispers of Paradise (1):

A Muslim Woman's Life Journal

An Islamic Daily Journal Which Encourages Reflection & Rectification

Abu Alee ath-Thaqafee said: Abu Hafs used to say:
"The one who does not each moment weigh his situation and condition against the scale of the Book of Allaah and the Sunnah, and does not question his very footsteps, then he is not to be considered worthy."
(Seyaar 'Alaam an-Nubala: vol. 12, page 512)

12 Monthly calendar pages with beneficial quotations from Ibn Qayyim & *Daily journal page* based upon Hijree calendar(with corresponding C.E. dates)

Each daily journal page starts with one of the following:

-A Verse from the Noble Qur'aan
-An Authentic Narration of the Messenger of Allaah
-An Authentic Supplication
-A Beneficial Point from a Biography of the Early Generations
-A Beneficial Statement from One of the Well Known Scholars, Past or Present

Available: **Now** | price: **$25**
[New elegantly designed edition for each year]

Made in United States
Troutdale, OR
11/15/2023

14606694R00084